LEGACY OF FAITH

LEGACY OF FAITH

From Women of the Bible
to Women of Today

LYDIA BROWNBACK

P&R

PUBLISHING

P.O. BOX 817 • PHILLIPSBURG • NEW JERSEY 08865-0817

Scripture quotations are from The Holy Bible, New King James Version. Copyright © 1979, 1980, 1982, Thomas Nelson, Inc.

Italics in Scripture quotations indicate emphasis added.

Page design and typesetting by Lakeside Design Plus

Printed in the United States of America

Library of congress Cataloging-in-Publication Data

Brownback, Lydia, 1963-
    Legacy of faith : from women of the Bible to women of today / Lydia Brownback.
       p. cm.
  Includes bibliographical references and index.
  ISBN 0-87552-004-9 (pbk.)
  1. Women in the Bible. 2. Christian women — Religious life. I. Title.

BS575.B76 2002
220.9'2'082 — dc21   2001059100

For my mother,
Wilma Lorraine Grunert Brownback

Her children rise up and call her blessed . . .
"Many daughters have done well,
But you excel them all. . . ."
Give her of the fruit of her hands,
And let her own works praise her in the gates.
Proverbs 31:28–31

Contents

Foreword

*G*reat heavens, what remarkable women are to be found among the Christians!" Thus spoke Libanios, the pagan philosopher who taught rhetoric in ancient Antioch. Although he was no friend of Christianity, Libanios marveled at the fortitude of the females who claimed to be followers of Christ.

What Christian women did in those days was truly remarkable. In the face of hardship, persecution, and even death, they demonstrated the love of Christ through practical deeds of compassionate service. Showing great perseverance and force of character, they worked to establish caring Christian communities. They reared children, visited prisoners, housed strangers, fed the poor, nursed the sick, and buried the dead. And they did it all with thanksgiving, worshiping God in the beauty of his holiness. When we will see their like again?

One way to learn how to become a woman of God is to follow the example of great women in the faith. Of course, the best examples come from the true stories in the Bible. The book in your hands contains more than twenty biblical lessons about living for the glory of God. Some of the women in these pages were loyal to God's people (Rahab and Ruth). Others persevered in prayer (Hannah and Anna). Still others dedicated their lives to Christian service (Lydia) or showed extravagant love for Jesus Christ (Mary Magdalene). Each positive example is an inspiration to become a woman after God's own heart.

Not all the women of the Bible were spiritually successful. However, even their failures can be instructive. Thus, this book includes lessons on leaving the world behind and not looking back (Lot's wife), on being content with the position that God assigns (Miriam), on not manipulating people for evil purposes (Delilah), and on making the time to commune with Christ (Martha). Taken together, the good examples and the bad examples teach what to avoid as well as what to emulate.

I first met Lydia Brownback at Westminster Theological Seminary, where she was among the best students in her class. In this book, she has used her biblical training to good advantage, offering fresh perspectives on the most important women in the Bible. Each chapter is theologically informed and contains relevant information about the biblical and cultural context.

This is also a book that connects, applying biblical truth to the heart issues that real Christian women face every day. It deals with vital matters of faith and friendship, failure and fulfillment. My prayer is that as you read, you will aspire to live up to the high standard set by the great Christian women of the past.

Philip Graham Ryken
Senior Minister
Tenth Presbyterian Church
Philadelphia, Pennsylvania

Acknowledgments

God has greatly helped me understand his love, through not only the women in Scripture but also those through whom he has personally blessed me. Specifically I am grateful for the support and encouragement I received to pursue this project from Mina Brownback Hayn, Susan Flanigan, Karen Montgomery, Ruth Floyd Rush, and Sue Wilkey and the other members of my women's Bible study. I am indebted to my mother, Wilma Brownback, for laying aside her projects to provide me with editorial assistance. Finally, I am grateful to God for the example of love, commitment, and godliness he has given me through my best friend and sister, Elizabeth Renee Blackburn.

Introduction

$\mathcal{E}$verywhere we turn, we hear about what today's woman thinks and feels. Western women living at the onset of the twenty-first century, we are told, can embrace opportunities, ambitions, and successes like never before in history. In many ways that is true. Women today owe much to the feminist movement of the early twentieth century, the movement as it was prior to its trendy, militant form. We have unprecedented freedom of choice in matters of career, lifestyle, and marital status.

Yet in reality, women today, despite their freedom, experience all the same things as did their sisters down through the centuries. Our newfound freedoms have not alleviated loneliness, shame, failure, and heartbreak. We suffer as keenly as women in every age and society. In actuality, the potential for stress and anxiety has only increased, since along with greater freedom has come greater responsibility.

The grave error many women make today is believing the lie that we are more enlightened than women of previous centuries or those in less civilized countries. Educational opportunities abound in our culture like no other, yet the purest enlightenment comes not from any classroom or college course. It comes only from God's Word applied by the Holy Spirit. Where has that reliance gone? The answer is simple: Belief in Scripture as authoritative has been diminished greatly by an autonomous independence characterized by selfishness.

That is and has always been an unfortunate and all too frequent accompaniment to freedom.

If we are honest, we must admit that we are no happier than the women who lived such restricted lives before us in supremely male-dominated societies. All our freedom has not won for us true contentment and peace. That is because those traits can still be found only where they have always been found—through an acknowledgment of our sin and utter dependence on Jesus Christ as he is portrayed in God's Word.

In Scripture, we have the opportunity to discover how God has worked in and through women of varied circumstances. There we find them rich and poor, loved and unloved, of good repute and bad. We see women like Sarah and Hannah, who knew firsthand the anguish of infertility. There are women such as Rahab, who knew the humiliation of a shameful past. Others, like Miriam and Martha, struggled with problems arising from their assertive temperaments, always a catalyst of conflict, especially for the sex lauded for quiet deportment. There was Abigail, a graceful women trapped in a marriage to a boorish drunk. In Mary Magdalene we find a woman whose desire to love passionately found its eternal fulfillment in Jesus Christ.

This book contains a brief glimpse into twenty-four women found in Scripture. From each one we can learn about our relationship to God and how he uses the troubles and traits inherent to women to set us apart for himself. Although there are many valuable points to be gleaned from each of the twenty-four women, only one specific characteristic about each has been highlighted here. As you read about their lives, it is my hope that you will see, when the cultural veneer has been stripped away, that we share the same hopes and can lay claim to the same promises that they did, because God is the same yesterday, today, and forever.

1

Eve

The Tricks of Temptation

Saks vs. K-Mart

Who doesn't have at least one white cotton T-shirt? For old and young, male and female, work and weekend, T-shirts are a basic part of the American wardrobe. Sold on racks, in piles, and packages of three, lightweight, fine-gauge, scoop neck, V-neck, pocketed, or plain, T-shirts are items that clothing retailers keep in stock year round. Regardless of weight, style, and neckline differences, they are still just white cotton T-shirts. Why, then, are so many women spending fifty dollars for the Ralph Lauren version selling off a rack at Saks rather than grabbing a three-pack at K-Mart for so much less? It is because retailers understand that the average American mindset is easy prey to the power of suggestion. Successful advertisers have mastered that power—indeed, they have mastered us.

What images come to mind when you think of Ralph Lauren? Wealth, beautiful people, sexy smiles, toned bodies, trendsetters. K-Mart, on the other hand, smacks of middle-class practicality, a necessary slice of the mundane. Those particular images come to mind because advertisers want them to. When a woman purchases the fifty-dollar T-shirt, she is attempting to buy the aura that is marketed with it. Those who shop at K-Mart feel they have gotten a bargain, one up on the less thrifty. K-Mart shoppers are purchasing a sense of superiority and accomplishment. The power of suggestion works because it appeals to our lusts. In fact, it has worked so well that it now dominates our culture in every sphere of life.

No Trouble in Paradise

But this is nothing new. It goes back to the beginning of redemptive history in the Garden of Eden, where the first successful marketing representative was a serpent. It all began on a day much like any other in the garden. Adam was tending the landscape, with Eve helping him. There was plenty to eat and drink, and the two were living in unbroken fellowship with God. Their lives were peaceful because God had issued instructions for happy living in the garden. Adam and Eve had been given free rein to make use of everything there except for one solitary tree, the Tree of the Knowledge of Good and Evil. God had made clear that if they ate from that tree, they would surely die. They were, however, free to enjoy the remainder of the garden's variety. It was into this perfect setting that Satan, disguised as a serpent, came to appeal to Eve's lusts.

A look at Eve's life makes us wonder why she would have been susceptible to temptation, what unmet longings could be cultivated into lustful cravings. At that time her life was absolutely perfect. God had provided her with everything she needed. Unlike us, she had no financial worries or clothing concerns. She had no relational problems. As of yet there were no children to rear. Eve's sole task was enjoying life in the garden in the company of God and Adam. God had seen to her well-being in every way. Eve had no excuse to sin.

But lest we be too quick to pass judgment on Eve, we should remember that, in spite of our troubles, we have no more excuse for our sin than she had. We often look for excuses and extenuating circumstances on which to place the blame for what we do. We point to relational problems, financial struggles, hormones, overwork, and unmet desires of one sort or another. Our excuses are endless. But we do not need to let those things trick us into sin, because God provides for the complete welfare of his women today, just as he did for Eve. The Bible tells us, "His divine power has given to us all things that pertain to life and godliness, through the knowledge of Him who called us by glory and virtue" (2 Peter 1:3). Therefore, since we have been given all we need, our troubles need never be the cause for sin, any more than they were for Eve.

Underlying Issues

So, since difficult circumstances did not lead Eve to fall, what did? She sinned for the same reason that we do—she wanted something that she did not have.

> Now the serpent was more cunning than any beast of the field which the LORD God had made. And he said to the woman, "Has God indeed said, 'You shall not eat of every tree of the garden'?" And the woman said to the serpent, "We may eat the fruit of trees of the garden; but of the fruit of the tree which is in the midst of the garden, God has said, 'You shall not eat it, nor shall you touch it, lest you die.' " (Gen. 3:1–3)

The first thing the serpent did was to set Eve thinking about the one thing she did not have. He attempted to get her eyes off her blessings and plant the idea of deprivation. Temptation comes to us in precisely the same way, and when it does, it causes us to question the goodness of God and the truth of his words.

A young woman who attends my church, Rachel, signed up to travel with the missions team to Brazil. Each participant was responsible for raising his or her financial support to go along; so to prepare, Rachel placed herself on a strict budget. Off limits were any new clothes, meals out with friends, and other nonessentials. Shortly afterward, Rachel received an invitation to a formal dinner dance that she eagerly accepted. As the date of the dance grew near, Rachel grew anxious about what to wear, and as she assessed her closet, nothing seemed right. Oh, she had appropriate attire hanging inside, but she had worn all those outfits countless times before.

Rachel began to reassess the terms of her newly established budget. Would a one-time exception really be a setback? "After all," she reasoned, "this was to be a very special occasion. Furthermore," she thought, "the missions trip is for the good of others. I can do something good for myself, too, since I am making a sacrifice to go to Brazil." She also reinforced her determination to compromise by looking away from God: "The Bible tells me I needn't bother stressing myself over clothing because God will take care of me, but the Bible doesn't guarantee that God will make me look good—I need a special new outfit to accomplish that!"

This is how temptation works within us, and once it has taken root we stop looking at all that God has provided for us. Instead, we begin to focus on what we are lacking or on what we feel we deserve. Questioning the goodness of God and the Word of God always lies at the root of temptation.

Strategic Warfare

Eve also attempted to reason against temptation. Rather than shutting her mind to the serpent's suggestion, she engaged him in conversation. But since the enemy was more cunning that Eve, and a lot smarter, it was a fatal mistake. If we stop to converse with the enemy—even in the form of argument—half the battle is lost. For one thing, it is an indicator that we are already considering what is being proffered. Additionally, we cannot outwit temptation merely by the strength of our own minds and hearts. We are not up to the task.

So if argument does not work, what does? It is so easy to get frustrated in our battles against sin! What works is what Jesus did when he was tempted by the devil in the wilderness: "Now when the tempter came to Him, he said, 'If you are the Son of God, command that these stones become bread.' But He answered and said 'It is written, "Man shall not live by bread alone, but by every word that proceeds from the mouth of God" ' " (Matt. 4:3–4).

Both Eve and Jesus were tempted by food, but the difference was that Eve stood in the midst of abundant nourishment, whereas Jesus had not eaten anything for forty days. In both cases, Satan cleverly tried to get their eyes off of God and onto themselves. He did not succeed with Jesus, but Eve was caught because she failed to rely solely on God's words. The greatest difference in Eve and Jesus' responses was that Jesus trusted the Word of God and Eve did not. That means that if Jesus relied on Scripture to resist the wiles of the devil, how much more must we! From Jesus' experience we learn that God's Word is the only viable weapon on which to rely for victory, but it is a strong weapon indeed.

At that point temptation took a greater hold on Eve, and she began to attribute mean qualities to God. She said to the serpent, "God has said, 'You shall not eat it, nor shall you touch it, lest you die' " (Gen. 3:3). However, if you look at what God said (Gen. 2:16–17), you will see that he never stated that they could not touch the tree but only that they must not eat from it. Have you fallen into that trap? It happens when we waltz around a sinful suggestion, toying with it in our minds. Suddenly God's commands seem petty and restrictive. In our thinking God takes on the aspect of a tyrant, one who demands proof of loyalty by means of personal deprivation. That is exactly how Eve came to think, and it took only a subtle insinuation to accomplish it.

As the destructive dialogue continued, the serpent exerted his advantage with outright lies. He said, "You will not surely die. For God knows that in the day you eat of it your eyes will be opened, and you will be like God, knowing good and evil" (Gen. 3:4–5). Careful insinuation and subtle suggestion were no longer necessary. In essence, he said, "Look here, Eve. God said you would die, but that was just to scare you. What he really knows—but didn't let you in on—is that you'll be more fulfilled as a person if you eat from this tree. God doesn't want you to experience personal fulfillment, Eve. He wants to keep you down so he can control you. He knows that if you eat the fruit you'll be independent, in control of your own life. Why should God have all the power? Don't you want to be like him?"

Who's the Boss?

Succumbing to the temptation for such autonomy is the greatest of all evils. In desiring to raise ourselves up in independence from God, we are seeking to displace him from power. As horrible as it sounds, as much as we cringe at hearing it, at the root of such independence is the desire for the death of God. Such a desire is pride in its purest form, and it is a desire that lurks in every human heart, including mine and yours, even after we are saved. This most sinful of sins is more destructive than anything else imaginable. It is what got Satan kicked out of heaven. It is what drove King Nebuchadnezzar to insanity. It is what caused the crucifixion of Jesus Christ. And we are all guilty of it. Oh, we do not consciously think or say that we want to be like God, but the desire is there in our hearts nevertheless. In every sin we commit, we are declaring our desire for independence, autonomy, and control over our lives. It was the ultimate hook on which to snag Eve, and it is the hook that grabs us as well.

The New Testament tells us, "For all that is in the world—the lust of the flesh, the lust of the eyes, and the pride of life—is not of the Father but is of the world" (1 John 2:16). When Eve saw that the tree was good for food (the lust of the flesh), that is was pleasant to the eyes (the lust of the eyes), and that it was a tree desirable to make one wise (the pride of life), she took of its fruit and ate (not of the Father but of the world). Can you see that chain of events in the things that tempt you? It is there in the little things as well as the big. We are all prone to lusts of one sort or another. They are often desires for good things that, when overemphasized, turn into intense cravings that rage within us. If these desires are left unchecked, it is most often the case that we succumb and fall into sin. That is what Eve did, and shame, misery, and death resulted.

A Redeemer to the Rescue

But God did not leave Eve to get herself out of trouble, nor does he leave us. Afterward God came looking for Eve and her husband, and when they failed to come forth and greet him, he called out for them. But their guilty consciences cringed from exposure. Isn't that how you feel after you have sinned? Facing God is so hard because we are ashamed. We think we need to find a way to fix things first, or at least to try to minimize our shame and guilt. Eve was attempting to do that as she wrapped herself in fig leaves. But Eve did not have to hide and neither do we. God comes seeking us. He calls us back to himself. If you have been redeemed by the blood of Christ, you never have to fear that your sin drives God away from you. If you feel that he has left, it is an illusion created by your sense of failure and guilt. God is still beside you, and more so, he does all the work in reconciling you to himself, just as he did for Eve in the garden.

Jesus said, "What man of you, having a hundred sheep, if he loses one of them, does not leave the ninety-nine in the wilderness, and go after the one which was lost until he finds it? And when he has found it, he lays it on his shoulders, rejoicing. And when he comes home, he calls together his friends and neighbors, saying to them, 'Rejoice with me, for I have found my sheep which was lost!' " (Luke 15:4–6).

God also knows that, as we face him with our failure, we will be tempted to pass the blame off on someone or something else, because we are afraid of punishment. That is what happened in the garden when God came to restore his fallen children. "Then the man said, 'The woman whom You gave to be with me, she gave me of the tree, and I ate.' And the LORD God said to the woman, 'What is this you have done?' The woman said, 'The serpent deceived me, and I ate' " (Gen. 3:12–13). Adam blamed Eve; Eve blamed the serpent. If you have played the blame game, know that you are not alone. It is instinctive to our sin nature, evidenced in the fact that its tactics are employed even by small children.

However, as adults our finger pointing is more sophisticated than when one child points to another, declaring, "She did it!" Our blame passing goes more like this: "I could love others—if only God would provide someone to love me first." Or, "How can you expect me to me joyful when my husband is always in a bad mood?" And, "You'd struggle with patience too if you had the co-workers I have!" How about, "Life is way too stressful to lose this extra weight. I can't possibly diet right now." That is sophisticated blame shifting, echoes of Eve. Do you recognize this line of thinking in yourself? If you are like most of us, you will. We are afraid to take responsibility for our sins.

But the good news of the gospel is that you have nothing to fear if you have been redeemed by Jesus Christ. That is because he has already suffered the punishment for all your sins—past, present, and future. We may still suffer as a consequence of our sin; however, when that happens, it is God's loving discipline rather than wrathful justice. A good parent does not spank her child in anger; rather, she does it to turn the child away from a destructive path. Just so with God. Even the consequences of our sin are all regulated by him for our good.

That doesn't mean that our sins are brushed aside by God. Far from it! In fact, the price Jesus paid for our sins was insurmountably high. It cost him his life, which was taken from him by means of a bloody, ugly death. Such a death was necessary, because the shedding of blood is always required to take away sin. That was just as true for Eve's sin as it is for your sin and mine, and Jesus paid for her sin just as he did for ours. But since Jesus had not yet come to redeem us, God prefigured Christ's sacrifice on Eve's behalf in another way.

The story tells us, "Also for Adam and his wife the LORD God made tunics of skin, and clothed them" (Gen. 3:21). How could animal skins provide atonement for sin? Think about what is involved in the process of obtaining animal skins. An animal must first be slaughtered, and when that happens blood is shed. God came and took away the guilt of their sin. He then covered their nakedness, their shame, with his provision of righteousness. God did all the work. Eve did not have to earn her way back after succumbing to temptation.

You may be weighed down with the guilt of some sin, something that is keeping you from turning back to God. If so, you need not hide, because Jesus Christ has already paid for your failure. Get up and go back, keeping in mind all that Jesus has done for you. When you do, you'll find what Eve did—that God has already come to meet you, not with retribution but with love and blessing.

2

Sarah

Worth the Wait

Promises . . . Promises

Promises, vows, and commitments—so easily made, so easily broken—leave us leaning on the tottering leg of good intentions. The politician who vows not to raise taxes, the father who promises his son a game of catch after dinner, or the bride and groom who stand at the altar. How easily such promises are cast aside when distractions or discomforts come around. Is there anyone we can count on? We've been let down by those we trust most, and unquestionably we've broken our word to others. Even when keeping our word is within our power, we so easily break our promises when sticking by them doesn't suit us.

Not so with God. He never breaks his word or fails to do all he says. God's promises are infinite. All we have to do is open the Bible to find one. Whatever our need, there is a promise perfectly suited for its provision.

What promises do you need? Perhaps you are lonely. If so, open your Bible to Psalm 68:6, and you'll discover God's promise to provide for those who are alone. Is your conscience weighed down by guilt? First John contains God's promise of complete forgiveness through Christ Jesus. Are you struggling to overcome a sinful habit? If so, Romans 6:14 gives a tremendous promise that sin has no dominion over Christ's people. Is it a question of guidance? Turn to Proverbs 3:5–6 or Psalm 139, and you'll see that God has a path already marked out for you. He promises to guide those who are willing to go wherever he leads. Yet in light of those promises—and thousands more—why do we so often doubt? It's not as if God were unreliable like us!

Sarah's Struggle

A look at the Old Testament matriarch Sarah will help us answer this question. Who was Sarah? She was the wife of Abraham, as well as his half-sister. She'd come with her husband to the land of Canaan when God called them out of their homeland, Ur. Throughout her married life she suffered the plight of so many women: she wanted children but was unable to conceive.

Do you know a woman in that situation? If so, you've likely witnessed grief and sorrow as the years roll by and she relinquishes her maternal dreams and instincts. In all of the many difficulties Sarah experienced during her life with Abraham, her barrenness was perhaps the greatest hardship of all those years.

Infertility is common even in this age of advanced technology and medical experts. So many of us know one or more women facing childlessness. Bearing no children was even more difficult in Sarah's day. In the ancient Near East, a woman's social status and security were largely determined by the number of sons she produced. Bearing sons was a guarantee of respect and favor within the community. Back then, sons were obligated to provide for their parents in old age, so a woman with many sons faced comfortable elderly years.

However, even in this age of Social Security benefits and female self-sufficiency, for the woman who desires children but does not have them, there is often deep heartache. Sarah had no reason to ache, though, because God had promised that she would bear her husband a child.

Sarah's thoughts, feelings, and spiritual outlook, as shown to us, are those of a woman who had already lived for ninety years. What we quickly discover about Sarah is that although she had faith in God and had been given specific promises of future blessing, she nevertheless doubted God's ability to fulfill his word. Doubt had characterized her outlook for several years, as we can see by tracing her story in Genesis.

It began years before when God had appeared to Abraham and promised him a vast multitude of descendants (Gen. 15:3–5). But as time rolled forward, no child was forthcoming. Sarah lost hope in the Lord's promise, and as her doubt intensified into discouragement, she took matters into her own hands.

Sarah took charge by employing a practice common in many cultures of the time. A barren woman often achieved motherhood vicariously through a household slave. The husband would impregnate the servant, and the subsequent child was given to the wife to rear as her own. Sarah decided that this was the only realistic solution to her problem. In reality, it was the only *visible* solution.

Sarah cajoled her husband, "See now, the LORD has restrained me from bearing children. Please, go in to my maid; perhaps I shall obtain children by her" (Gen. 16:2). We could attribute her sinful action to impatience, but more likely it was rooted in a lack of faith. As a result of diminished trust in God, Sarah probably convinced herself that this sinful remedy was how God had intended to fulfill his promise. So Abraham impregnated Sarah's maid, Hagar, who bore him a son, Ishmael.

That's what happens when we place too much emphasis on our circumstances. We stop seeing the true God and his ways clearly. Although God's initial promise of descendants for Abraham made no mention of Sarah personally, that should have been assumed, because deriving offspring through a slave was a deviation from God's design for marriage (Gen. 2:23–24). Sarah and Abraham would have known that.

If she'd only kept her eyes on God, how much more peace Sarah's household would have known! Her actions resulted in great heartache for herself, her husband, her maid, Hagar, and the resulting child, Ishmael. Naturally, jealousy sprang up between the two women, and great strife dominated the household. Sarah's remedy had failed miserably.

It was fourteen years after Sarah's unfortunate choice that the Angel of the Lord came back to repeat God's promise of descendants. Although the Angel again directed his words to Abraham, Sarah could hear for herself this time because she was nearby preparing food in the tent. Outside, where the Angel was speaking with her husband, Sarah overheard him say, "I will certainly return to you according to the time of life, and behold, Sarah your wife shall have a son" (Gen. 18:10). In spite of Sarah's years of doubt, in spite of her sinful mishandling of God's decree, the Angel had come to encourage the couple and dispel their unbelief.

Seeing Is Believing?

How do you imagine an infertile woman would respond to such a promise? If she knows our loving and all-powerful God, her sorrow would vanish straight away. But Sarah's reaction was not what we'd expect. She laughed. Not a joyful laughter, but rather one born of scornful cynicism, a reaction that reveals continuing doubt in God and his promises.

But can we criticize Sarah for doubting? On the one hand, practical, rational thinking dictated that there was no way she could physically have a child. She'd been barren since her wedding day—was she now to conceive as a ninety-year-old woman? On the other hand, the Lord had come issuing a specific promise for that very thing.

Sarah doubted because she chose to doubt by focusing on her circumstances rather than on God and his words. If her vision had been God-centered, the nature of her laughter would have been different; it would have contained joyful anticipation of the Lord's blessing rather than cynicism.

The same is true of us. Do you realize that every time you experience doubt, it is because you are looking at your circumstances rather than at the promises of God in Scripture? Doubt is a direct response to looking away from God. If your circumstances are what you focus on, they will dictate how you think.

Well, what did the Angel do when Sarah laughed? Her laughter wasn't audible, but the Angel, because he was really the Lord, heard it. He didn't withdraw his promise or rebuke her for doubting; rather, after repeating his promise, he employed a tactic found frequently in Scripture. He asked her a question to redirect her thoughts. He asked, "Is anything too hard for the LORD?" (Gen. 18:14). The Angel was seeking to bring Sarah's attention back to the reality of God's power and away from her frail body. If she'd only keep her eyes on God, she would remember that he can and would do everything he had promised.

Skeptics in Scripture

Sarah was not the only doubter found in the Bible. Moses is another one. After Moses had led the Israelites out of Egypt and into the desert, the Lord caused him to confront his doubts. While in the wilderness, Moses faced a tough challenge. After more than two years of leading God's people, Moses had grown discouraged. The Israelite tribe, for which he was responsible, complained bitterly in its desert circumstances, and the negative attitude of the people disheartened Moses tremendously (see Num. 11).

Rather than laughing cynically, however, Moses took his discouragement to God, who offered him immediate help. But in spite of God's specific promise, Moses still doubted. He had his eyes fixed on his surroundings, so he couldn't imagine how God could possibly fulfill his word. But just as God had done with Sarah, he refocused Moses' gaze by getting him to think. "Has the LORD's arm been shortened?" God asked him (Num. 11:23). In other words, "Is the Lord's power limited?" He wanted Moses to think about all he knew of God from

all God had done for him in times past. Had God ever failed to provide a timely answer? If Moses would reflect on God's past provision,
he'd have confidence for the future, as well.

The prophet Jeremiah is another example of someone placed in
difficult circumstances. He, too, grew discouraged while waiting for
God to act. Jeremiah had done everything God instructed, but the
results he desired were not forthcoming. You can read about how the
prophet handled his doubts in Jeremiah 32. In essence Jeremiah
prayed, "God, I know that you can do anything. Why then are you
not doing what you promised?" God answered Jeremiah by posing the
same question he had asked Sarah and Moses years earlier: "Behold
[in other words, look at me], "I am the LORD, the God of all flesh. Is
anything too hard for Me?" (Jer. 32:27).

Jesus' disciple, Peter, doubted, and it got him into trouble. We read
in Matthew 14 that Jesus commanded Peter to walk toward him on
top of the water—a physically impossible task. All the while that
Peter kept his eyes fixed on Jesus, he was able to do the impossible.
But as soon as he looked away from his Master and saw the stormy
water churning beneath his feet, he began to sink. In spite of Peter's
doubt, Jesus didn't leave him to drown. That's because the fulfillment
of God's promises does not depend on us. It depends on him. However, Jesus did rebuke Peter, just as he had Sarah and the others. While
Jesus helped him up out of the waves he said, "O you of little faith,
why did you doubt?" (Matt. 14:31).

Doubt, Discouragement, and Despair: A Deadly Trio

God knows we get discouraged, but he also knows we have no reason to doubt because he will always provide what we need. Discouragement, the sister of doubt, is never necessary for those of us who
belong to Jesus Christ. From Peter, Jeremiah, Moses, and Sarah, we
learn that the way out of such negativity lies in taking our thoughts
straight to God and keeping them centered there.

Since discouragement comes when we allow doubt to dominate our thinking, it stands to reason that discouragement left to fester eventually leads to despair. Have you experienced this downward spiritual spiral? Have you grown weary of waiting for one of God's promises to come to pass in your life? If so, how are you handling your thoughts? If you are doubting God's goodness, or ability, or willingness to bless you, take those doubts straight to him. Doing so sooner rather than later prevents depression.

As with Sarah, if we don't do that we are easily tempted to seek our own way out of difficulty. With her eyes fixed on circumstances—her aging body, Abraham's old age, her lifetime of barrenness—Sarah couldn't imagine God being able to keep his promise. Rather than looking to God and trusting him, she attempted to manufacture fulfillment of her hope by taking control of her circumstances in a manner clearly outside of God's instruction. Her first failure led to the sinful creation of a self-made remedy, a snare we, too, must guard against. If we attempt to get what we want outside of God's ways, we'll find what Sarah did—that our own devices offer no permanent solutions to what troubles us. This is a truth we often learn only after repeated attempts have failed to get us what we want.

Control That Leads to Chaos

Considering your own life, think carefully about the following questions. Have you ever tried to escape doubts or discouragement by racing ahead of God? Perhaps there has been something in your life for which you've waited for God's provision for a very long time. While waiting did you cling unswervingly to his Word, or did you become fixated on your problem, thus making room for doubts to creep in? Did you become desperate for a solution? Did you look around at what you could do to solve your problem yourself, to fulfill your dream, perhaps reasoning from circumstances that a particular course of action was within God's will, even if that path contradicted Scripture? If you did that, what was the result? Did your plans work out? Did jumping ahead of God bring you what you had hoped for? Very likely, you cannot say "yes" with absolute surety.

I learned this lesson before I began to work in full-time Christian ministry. For years, laboring in ministry was one of the greatest desires of my heart. I graduated from seminary hopeful and full of anticipation for the doors God would open, but a year later I was still working in a job that I did not like while waiting for an opportunity. Doubt grew, and I began to wonder if I'd been mistaken in what I believed God had gifted me to do. Doubt grew into discouragement, and on the brink of despair, I took matters into my own hands.

Deciding to live off my savings, I quit my job to devote all my energies to opening a door to full-time Christian work. For the following three months I contacted countless ministries and wrote dozens of letters, all the while asking God to bless the effort. But no doors opened. It was not God's timing. You can probably guess what happened. I ran out of money and was forced to go back to full-time work in a secular setting. Once back in the workplace, I decided I should let go of my hope. I reasoned that I had merely mistaken personal desire for the call of God on my life. However, one year later I received a call from a Christian organization I'd written to, not during my frantic search but long before then. Not only did that ministry offer me a position far better than any I'd hoped for, but it also opened up doors to ministry opportunities that had not existed the year before.

God is good, and his timing is perfect. I see now that setting out on my own was merely a self-focused attempt to escape my depression and an unwillingness to live for God where he wanted me at that time. Therein lies a valuable lesson: When it is God's time to act, nothing will stand in his way. When we try to get ahead of him, we'll find the road rocky and usually unsuccessful. If I had renewed my trust by focusing on his Word, I'd still have ended up working in that ministry but likely with a lot more money in the bank and more peace in my heart along the way.

You do not have to test that for yourself, however. Instead, you can learn in Scripture, from the life of Sarah, that answers to prayer are often slow in coming and are revealed over a long period of time.

Worth the Wait

Sarah waited fourteen years after the birth of the misbegotten Ishmael before God fulfilled his promise to her. "And the LORD visited Sarah as He had said, and the LORD did for Sarah as He had spoken. For Sarah conceived and bore Abraham a son in his old age, at the set time of which God had spoken to him" (Gen. 21:1–2).

The child of promise was given the name of Isaac. That name means "laughter," and it was the name God had chosen for the child (Gen. 17:19). Isaac's name would forever after serve as a reminder to Sarah and Abraham that God is the God who turns cynical laughter into the laughter of joy.

However, we must not overlook that Sarah's former cynicism had displeased God. When the Angel had stood outside Sarah's tent and reaffirmed God's promise of descendants, Sarah's scornful response was no small matter in his eyes. The Lord said to Abraham, "Why did Sarah laugh, saying, 'Shall I surely bear a child, since I am old?' Is anything too hard for the LORD?" . . . But Sarah denied it, saying, "I did not laugh," for she was afraid. And He said, "No, but you did laugh!" (Gen. 18:13–15)

God takes doubting very seriously. It is indeed no small thing. It dishonors him, and as we've seen, doubt unchecked leads to discouragement, and he would spare us that. When we trust in God's willingness and ability to keep his promises, he is glorified and we are peaceful.

Look at the difference in Sarah's attitude fourteen years later: "And Sarah said, 'God has made me laugh, and all who hear will laugh with me.' She also said, 'Who would have said to Abraham that Sarah would nurse children? For I have borne him a son in his old age' " (Gen. 21:6–7). The name Isaac was to serve as a reminder that a cynical attitude displeases God, because he is worthy of Sarah's trust, and ours too. God also knows that when we persevere in faith, the outcome will always be joy.

Root Out Your Doubt

The New Testament epistle of James gives us a strong warning about doubt. James wrote, "But let him ask in faith, with no doubting, for he who doubts is like a wave of the sea driven and tossed by the wind. For let not that man suppose that he will receive anything from the Lord; he is a double-minded man, unstable in all his ways" (James 1:6–7).

It is not that God is unwilling to give but rather that we are unable to receive his gifts. We are too busy looking at ourselves and our circumstances to see what God has for us. That is why receiving God's gifts is possible only from a position of trust. If our eyes are fixed solely on what we want, we cannot receive what God is offering.

Sarah overcame her doubts by accepting the rebuke of the Angel. We don't read about that in Genesis but only much later in the New Testament letter to the Hebrews. It says, "By faith Sarah herself also received strength to conceive seed, and she bore a child when she was past the age, because she judged Him faithful who had promised" (Heb. 11:11). Sarah got her eyes off her circumstances and onto God, and the resulting trust was the vehicle God used to enable her to conceive. Doubt leads only to the loss of power. Faith always supplies it.

Are you doubting God? Have you been discouraged? Take your doubts, concerns, and fears to God in prayer. Then get your eyes off yourself by immersing your mind in the promises found in his Word. You'll discover that the right focus leads to the right perspective, and your cynical laughter, like Sarah's, will turn into the laughter of joy.

3

Hagar

Where Freedom Is Found

It's Not Fair!

I recently met a woman experiencing the joy of newfound freedom. Her name is Emily, and for the first time in seven years she feels unburdened. Attempting to rear two children virtually alone has left her exhausted, frustrated, and angry at her husband's inability to hold a job. Now that she's found the courage to leave him and move back in with her parents, she has built-in child care and some hours of much needed solitude to figure out what lies ahead for herself and her children.

When Emily first met Bob he seemed ambitious, and his career in advertising looked promising. But right after the birth of their first child, Lee, Bob was let go in a companywide layoff. Bob's role as provider for his young family was threatened. Added to that was the adjustment of sharing his wife with the demands of a newborn. Bob began to resent the hours of each day and night Emily spent with Lee. Over time, his efforts at finding a new and satisfying job faded, until Bob was forced by financial constraints to take a lesser position in a small advertising agency. The agency folded just after the arrival of their second child, Lyle, and so did Bob's ambition. He became more and more withdrawn from Emily as she devoted the time necessary to caring for two young children.

For the next several years, Bob could be found most often on the couch, television blaring. He was quiet and withdrawn, uninvolved with Emily and the children. The family was forced to accept financial assistance from Emily's parents again and again, deepening Bob's depression and embarrassing Emily. Finally Emily threatened to leave with the children, so Bob agreed to get help. Together they met with their pastor, who helped them make some plans to break the downward spiral of their marriage. Emily accepted a full-time secretarial job after Bob promised to become a fully involved, stay-at-home parent. Perhaps they'd all function best this way, Emily thought. Lots of families were trying these arrangements with great success.

Emily was euphoric over the next few weeks. Bob had come to life. When she'd get home from work, dinner was cooked and the children were fed, and Bob took an active interest in her daily tasks. Perhaps things were going to work out fine after all. But after that first month, Bob's familiar pattern began to emerge. Stacks of dirty dishes, unwashed clothes, and crying children in need of attention awaited Emily every evening. Tears and the television were her homecoming at the end of each workday.

Bolstered by her newfound independence to provide income for the family, Emily came home one evening, packed a few necessary things for the children and herself, and left her husband. "I'm tired of this life!" she told him. "We are not a team. I do everything while you sit around and sponge off of my paycheck! If you loved me and the children, you'd deal with your depression and get on with living our life together. But you haven't, and you won't, and I can't take it any longer!"

Now, as Emily rests in the relief she feels outside the gloom of her married home life, she begins to anticipate a new beginning. She thinks of what life will be like without the weight of Bob and his moodiness, his laziness, and his resentment toward her when she isn't focused exclusively on him. "There's no limit now," she thinks. "I can begin again, perhaps even meet someone new, a man with the ambition Bob once had."

Not many days went by before Emily received a phone call from her pastor. Would she be willing for him to drop by and see her that evening? Emily accepted, eager to receive support and vindication for the bold move she had made. But she was not prepared for the pastor's words. He had come to show her all the Bible says about marriage, and the message is clear: If she wants to please God, she must go back to Bob. Or if she chooses to stay separated, she must remain faithful to him. The pastor reminded her of her marriage vows: till death us do part.

Emily was devastated, her newfound hopes dashed. Go back to Bob? Back to the endless monotony of a dead marriage?

"How can I?" Emily thought. "I don't even love him anymore. It's not fair!"

Emily is left with a choice: Obey the Bible, or take the road that appears to offer freedom and a new chance at happiness. A choice we all face at one time or another, and one made especially hard for women today. That's because we live in an era that rests more comfortably than ever before on the foundation of personal freedom.

Fixated on Freedom

Western women fought hard through the twentieth century to better their conditions in every sphere of life. As a result, we have a voice in choosing our elected officials, a diversity of career opportunities, and the luxury of choosing a lifestyle of singleness or marriage. These were hard-won battles, and we all enjoy the resulting benefits in some form or fashion, whether or not we are conscious of them on a daily basis. Women today enjoy a freedom in living as never before in human history.

However, for Christian women, there are negative repercussions, as well. To be a successful woman by contemporary standards often stands in opposition to success as defined by Scripture. The new freedoms have resulted in a compromised femininity, and Christian women have shown signs of succumbing in recent decades. Even as Christians, when we read or hear about anything that appears to limit our rights, our equality, our freedom, we are inclined toward a defensive mindset. We will do anything to preserve this new independence because we've come to believe that abdicating it will rob us of happiness.

Women walk out of marriages, terminate pregnancies, and preach from the pulpit—all in the name of equality and the right to happiness—regardless of Scripture's teaching on what truly makes them happy and free. We've lost sight of the fact that equality is not a biblical principle but rather a democratic one. Perhaps that's why, when we read the story of Hagar in Genesis, we are quick to react in indignation to her situation.

Hagar's Hindrance

Hagar, an Egyptian girl, was a bondservant, the personal maid of Abraham's wife, Sarah. Abraham likely acquired the girl while in Egypt.

When we looked at Sarah in the last chapter we discovered that her doubt in God's promises led her to take matters into her own hands. As we examine Hagar, we'll see how Sarah's sin set in motion a whole string of consequences, many of which directly affected the life of her maid, Hagar. Sarah's doubt in God's ability to give her a child of her own led her to seek the fulfillment of her desire through Hagar: "So Sarai said to Abram, 'See now, the LORD has restrained me from bearing children. Please, go in to my maid; perhaps I shall obtain children by her' " (Gen. 16:2).

We hear so much about women's rights to do what they wish with their bodies, even if that entails murdering another human being. But in the ancient Near East, women, regardless of social status, had little control over the circumstances of their lives, and women of the servant class had almost none.

So feeling sympathy for Hagar is our natural reaction. She was forced to have sex with a man not her husband, then had to endure the trials of pregnancy and painful childbirth, only to relinquish the infant to another woman to nurture. There is nothing we could call "fair" about that.

No Solution in Sin

We have to keep in mind, however, that Hagar had a very different view of that situation than we do. Considering the custom of the time, she likely considered herself fortunate. Being chosen to bear the child of the family patriarch was a great honor and would have bettered Hagar's lot significantly, were it not for the sinful way she acted when she found herself pregnant.

Hagar developed what we would call an "attitude problem," and it shows up in Genesis 16:4: "When [Hagar] saw that she had conceived, her mistress became despised in her eyes." Hagar felt superior to Sarah because she, a mere maid, could give Abraham a child, while Sarah, the cherished and favored wife, could not. As we read on through the story, it is evident that her attitude was not hidden from Sarah, and Sarah was overcome with rage and jealousy. It's easy, isn't it, to feel no pity for Sarah? After all, she brought the whole thing on herself. Mercifully, God is much more charitable toward us than we are toward each other!

Nevertheless, both women suffered the consequences of their respective sins. Sarah, in her jealousy, tried to manipulate her husband against Hagar, but he wanted no part of their bitter rivalry and washed his hands of the situation. He sinned in failing to take his rightful responsibility for the peace and well-being of his household: "So [Abraham] said to [Sarah], 'Indeed your maid is in your hand; do to her as you please.' And when [Sarah] dealt harshly with her, she fled from her presence" (Gen. 16:6).

How easily the sin of one individual inflames the sinful nature of another! Sarah's string of sinful events—mistrusting God, then cajol-

ing her husband to commit adultery—triggered Abraham's sin. He
conceded to Sarah's plan, which served as the catalyst for Hagar's
sin—her attitude problem with Sarah. Sarah then mistreated Hagar,
and on and on it went until God graciously intervened.

Yet God waited until Hagar had run away from home. Apparently
the abuse Sarah leveled at Hagar was severe enough to make the surrounding wilderness a more appealing choice than continued sub-
jection to her mistress. Either that, or Hagar's prideful attitude refused
to endure Sarah's authority. In either case, leaving the comforts of
food and shelter to undertake a solitary journey involving exposure
to the elements of the desert, wild animals and insects, and unreliable supplies of food and water—all while pregnant—indicates a desperate situation.

Regardless of her attitude, it is still easy for us to sympathize with
Hagar. After all, what is a bit of pride and an attitude problem when
compared with all Sarah had done to her? Now, here she is alone in
the wilderness with nowhere to go and no one to turn to. What would
you do if you found yourself in Hagar's situation? Would you journey
into the wilderness, risking your life and that of your unborn child?
Perhaps you would if you felt that doing so was your only good option.

Our Gracious Guide

It is here, at her point of desperation, that the Angel of the Lord
came to Hagar as she languished beside a spring of water in the wilderness on the way to Shur. The Angel said, "Hagar, Sarai's maid, where
have you come from, and where are you going?" (Gen. 16:8). Notice
the divine initiative. God always takes the first step to communicate
with us. Each and every time we pray, it is only because God, through
his Spirit, has first worked in our hearts to do so.

Note also how he addressed Hagar—gently and personally. God
desires an intensely personal relationship with all his people, and he
calls each one of us by name. If you take time to study the varied
occasions and people to whom God speaks throughout Scripture,

you'll find those instances characterized by kindness and personal involvement.

You'll also see how frequently God began his communications by questioning his listener. We see this in the case of Job, a man who railed against God in his suffering. Following a lengthy silence God answered Job. But he answered by asking the suffering man a series of penetrating questions (Job 38:2). You'll also find in the Gospels that Jesus began many of his parables that way, and he often countered the tricky questions of his critics with a trick question of his own. When Saul was stricken by Jesus on the road to Damascus, the striking was directly followed by a question: "Saul, Saul, why are you persecuting Me?" (Acts 9:4).

Let us not suppose that God lacks the answers. When he asked Hagar from where she had come and where she was going, God already knew everything about her circumstances. Rather, God's asking is an aspect of his gentleness with us; it is also a kind way to get us thinking in the direction he wants to take us.

In Hagar's case, that direction led back to Sarah as is evidenced from the fact that he addressed her as "Sarah's handmaid." He is carefully directing her thinking down the path he has marked out for her. In essence God is saying, "Hagar, I know you personally. I know your trials. I know how unfairly things have been going for you in the dwelling of Sarah and Abraham. I know why you ran away, and I know that you are suffering out here in the wilderness. You believe that anything is preferable to your situation back in that household. And since I know all of that, you can trust that I also know what's best for you to do."

God dealt with Hagar to make her receptive to his forthcoming instruction. The text says, "The Angel of the Lord said to her, 'Return to your mistress, and submit yourself under her hand' " (Gen. 16:9). He is not denying the validity of her suffering, nor does he promise that when she obeys, things will instantly become better. He merely makes clear what he wants her to do. Notwithstanding God's gentleness toward Hagar, the instruction was likely difficult for her to swallow. God didn't open up an exciting new opportunity or aid her in flight from her difficulties. The path of obedience was the least appealing option of all the competing alternatives that lay before her.

Obedience: The Path to Freedom

Before we look at Hagar's response, ask yourself what you would do in similar circumstances. Perhaps you find yourself seeking an escape from trouble or hardship. If so, does the escape you are contemplating jibe with Scripture and the advice of godly counselors? Perhaps you are unsure. If so, your immediate task is to commit to obedience with an open mind to going wherever God leads.

One alert to an unsurrendered heart is confusion. There is a confusion that stems from idolizing our desires. We may think we don't know what to do, when in reality the way is clearly marked out for us in Scripture. James 3:16 says, "For where envy and self-seeking exist, confusion and every evil thing will be there." Therefore, whenever we feel confused about a particular course, it is wise to pause and examine whether our confusion is caused by an inward demand to have our own way.

Minister and writer Donald Grey Barnhouse illustrated this principle well in a story he told frequently. One day his daughter came to him with a request that he denied. "Well, then, what do you want me to do?" she asked. He gave her his answer and went back to his work. But she remained standing in front of him. A few minutes later Mrs. Barnhouse called to the daughter from another room. "Where are you? What are you doing?" she asked. The daughter replied, "I am waiting for Daddy to tell me what he wants me to do." At this point, Barnhouse looked up from his work and said, "Whatever you are doing, you are not waiting to find out what I want you to do. I have told you what I want you to do, but you do not like it. You are actually waiting to see if you can get me to change my mind."[1]

How often we read God's Word selectively, tempted to disregard what doesn't make us feel better or lead us where we want to go!

Sometimes our discrimination is so subtle we aren't aware of it, which is why godly advice is crucial at times of extreme turmoil.

Light for Our Path

Scripture doesn't speak directly to some things, what we call gray areas, such as what job to take, or whether or not to marry a particular man, or whether to have a third child . But by studying what the Bible says in general, we will have the light we need for everything we face. The writer of Hebrews tells us, "For the word of God is living and powerful, and sharper than any two-edged sword, piercing even to the division of soul and spirit, and of joints and marrow, and is a discerner of the thoughts and intents of the heart" (Heb. 4:12).

Remember Emily. Returning to her marriage was the most unappealing of all the competing alternatives, yet it was the one marked out for her by Scripture. This is the point where we women fall easily into the rationalizations created by our culture regarding our rights. Societal pressures might tempt us, as they did Emily, to adopt the modern thinking that if she were to return to her marriage, it would inhibit her personal growth, or stifle her future opportunities, or quell her right to happiness. Yet the command stands: Go back, submit. Then trust God with the outcome.

We can learn a lot from Hagar's response, for not only did she get up and go; she also did so with a humble heart. She was delighted that the awesome God of the universe, the God of her master and mistress, had condescended to seek out a lonely and battered handmaiden to give her personal guidance (Gen. 16:13).

God also helped Hagar by holding out a promise of future blessing for her unborn son. And since Hagar was helped in her obedience by one promise, how much more should we be encouraged to obey with the countless promises given us in Scripture? When we obey, we'll learn what Hagar learned—that only by walking the path of obedience will we find blessing. And we can be sure we will, because God is faithful to his word.

4

Lot's Wife

The Eye of the Beholder

Personal Passions

Angela, Amy, Madeline, and Lynn are friends. Their lifestyles differ, but they know each from church and attend the same midweek Bible study. All four are busy, and for that reason they rarely see each other outside of church-related events.

Angela, age thirty, is a computer consultant for a large international accounting firm. She takes night classes to keep on the cutting edge of technology and to get ahead in her career. Three or four times a week, Angela is at the gym lifting weights or doing aerobics. Keeping up with current fashion trends is important to her, and since she's single, she can spend a hefty amount of her discretionary income on clothes, shoes, and fashion accessories. Angela has a passionate interest in the entertainment industry. She is always bubbling over with the latest tidbit of Hollywood gossip.

Amy is an attractive corporate attorney in her late-thirties. She is also single and is pursued romantically by the men at her firm. Amy has been devoting two evenings a week to learning to speak Italian to prepare for her upcoming vacation to Florence in two months. Her warm and friendly personality makes her popular wherever she goes. She would like to be married but hasn't met a compatible mate.

Madeline is in her thirties, but she is married and the mother of two girls. Her husband is a whiz in the financial industry, and his business acumen has placed the family in an income bracket rarely reached by most people, even in America. A live-in nanny and housekeeper have freed Madeline for participation in community activities and other volunteer projects. Much of Madeline's time is taken up with maintaining their large home and refurbishing their newly acquired weekend house at the beach.

Finally there is Lynn, a woman in her late twenties who desires more than anything to be an overseas missionary. Her job as church secretary doesn't pay much, which limits her participation in social activities. She lives simply in order to save the necessary funds to move overseas sometime during the next few years. Lynn's parents are dead, so she shares an apartment with her younger sister, who is finishing college. When she's not looking after her sister, Lynn is busy offering assistance and support to other missionaries with whom she keeps in contact. Lynn spends Friday evenings tutoring uneducated adults in English and basic math skills.

These four women hold in common their faith in Jesus Christ. Yet in spite of regular attendance at the Bible study over the past three years, their bond of faith has not led to deepened friendships. As much as Lynn enjoys the fellowship each Wednesday evening, she is bored by many of the activities that the others find stimulating. Conversely, Angela, Amy, and Madeline feel they cannot relate to Lynn. They find her commitment to missions rather intimidating. It requires so much personal sacrifice, something they do not wish to think about too much.

Yet despite Lynn's sacrifices, she is the most contented of the four. Angela is so wrapped up in trends, promotions, and keeping fit that she is often too busy to go to church. Being a trendsetter requires money, a well-toned body, and knowing what the up-and-coming fashions are, all of which take time and energy. Angela has worked hard to acquire her paycheck, her wardrobe, and her muscle tone. She does not want to contemplate anything that might require her to forego these accomplishments.

Amy derives her pleasure from the male attention she receives everywhere she goes, because deep down, Amy is lonely. She finds the company of high-powered businessmen stimulating. She has dated a few men from church, but in general she finds them a bit dull. Christian men are less apt to drop a bundle taking her to an exotic restaurant, and for the most part, they are much less sophisticated. Amy has always been attracted to men with a cosmopolitan flair, and since she has spent the majority of her social time in the company of unbelievers, she has trouble connecting socially with Christians.

Madeline's family and privileged lifestyle are not what inhibit a deep friendship with the other three women; rather, it is fear. Madeline is a worrier, always tense and anxious that something is going to go wrong. What if the money goes away? If the stock market takes a downturn, her husband's bonus check may decrease. One social blunder could shoot her social standing in the community. What will happen if she goes with her family to the church picnic instead of volunteering to help with the art museum charity ball? Madeline has trouble sleeping at night because she is afraid of losing all she has.

Why do you think Lynn is the most contented of these four Christian women? It is not because she is a missionary. It is not because she has been given a special capacity for contentment that the others lack. Rather, it is because her heart is set on things of lasting value, things that won't let her down; in essence, her heart is set on the things of God.

A Lot to Lose

Angela, Amy, and Madeline are much like Lot's wife, a woman we encounter briefly in the book of Genesis. We are never told her name; in the Bible she is referred to simply as Lot's wife. We are introduced to her while she and her family were living in the city of Sodom, an ancient settlement known for its decadence. Her husband, Lot, a nephew of Abraham, had initially been attracted to Sodom by its cosmopolitan aura, and it is likely that he met his wife after settling within the boundaries of the city. The Bible does not tell us whether she believed in God, but she had to know something about him since she had married a man who did.

Over time, Lot and his family had arrived at a place of prominence in the city. Genesis 19 tells us that Lot sat in the gate of the city, an honor reserved for men of high regard. They were recognized and established residents, a status that is typically achieved only through active participation and identification with other citizens. We are not told how Lot achieved his social standing. He may have acquired respect for his attempts at righteousness. More likely he had compromised with the world around him in order to obtain such a position. His wife may have come from a prominent family in Sodom, which would have conferred on Lot instant social status. We are not told. All we know is that Lot and his family were living quite successfully in this wicked city at the time God had appointed for its destruction. This ancient urban center had become a cesspool of corruption, sexual depravity, and godlessness. It was so evil that God determined to level it to ashes along with all its inhabitants.

Before destroying the city, however, God had determined to remove Lot and some of his family. To accomplish the rescue, God sent angels to lead them away from the coming judgment to a place of safety. Lot was sitting in the city gate when the angels, in the guise of men, arrived, and following the ancient customs of hospitality, Lot invited the angels to his home.

What did Lot's wife think about these two strangers? She apparently saw their arrival as an intrusion, for she did not extend to them gracious hospitality, unlike her husband. Lot was the one who welcomed the angels into their home and prepared a lavish meal. The Bible does not tell us what his wife was thinking about while Lot prepared the feast and served his guests. She may have been wondering, "What will my friends think? When will these strangers leave? Can we get them out before the neighbors notice?" Little did she realize that the situation was about to get much worse.

Later that evening, while the family and their guests were preparing for bed, the sound of voices surrounded the house. You can read about it in Genesis 19. The men of the city gathered at the door and demanded that Lot bring his guests outside. The evil men of Sodom were in a frenzy of lust, and they clamored to have sex with the two strangers. Lot, as host, had an obligation to protect his guests, and he did so at great peril to himself and his family. Lot slipped out the door to reason with the Sodomites.

He said, "Please, my brethren, do not do so wickedly! See now, I have two daughters who have not known a man; please, let me bring them out to you, and you do to them what you wish" (Gen. 19:7–8a). Lot's suggestion only incited the mob to fury, and they turned on him in an attempt to satiate their sexual lust. If the angels had not intervened it is likely that the family, its civic reputation notwithstanding, would have been murdered on the spot.

Lot's wife and daughters assuredly shuddered in fear at Lot's suggestion, but they would not have been as shocked by it as we would be. Back then, the obligations of the host to care for his guests superseded any other consideration. That was the customary practice among all honorable men.

Nevertheless, no one in the home was injured because the angels intervened and the evil men were thwarted. The family and its guests were safe for the night. During those dark hours, Lot, at the angels' insistence, urged his family to prepare for flight, but then he lay down to rest. When morning came, the angels urged Lot and his wife to arise and flee the city immediately. Destruction was coming! Indeed it was almost upon Sodom and its sister city, Gomorrah.

At this point, after all that had happened since the preceding day, Lot's wife should have been eager to go. Her family had been threatened by the very people with whom they associated every day. The cold and evil hearts hidden behind formerly smiling faces of neighbors and friends had been exposed to her in stark reality the night before. Her social standing was in ruin because her husband had denied the townsmen their demands. Furthermore, these two strange houseguests, men with an aura of authority, were urging her to flee from her home. Yet in spite of all that, she was hesitant to leave.

A Fork in the Road

Have you ever experienced this type of eye-opening incident, a pivotal time in your life when God opened your eyes to see something in all its ugliness, something formerly cloaked in the world's glamour? Were your eyes suddenly opened so that you could see something or someone—perhaps even a whole lifestyle—in a light different from what you had supposed it to be? If so, did the disillusionment turn you away from compromise and worldly ways? If it did, that was the grace of God helping you to safety. Unfortunately Lot's wife disregarded her opportunity.

The Bible tells us that she lingered. The angels had to take her by the hand and lead her forcibly from the city. If you belong to God, he will, if necessary, do the same for you. In his mercy, God will do whatever it takes to deliver his elect from danger. At times, he will also do that for those who are intimately connected with his chosen people, as was the case here during those early morning hours. We see that in Genesis 19:16, which tells us, "And while [Lot] lingered, the [angels] took hold of his hand, his wife's hand, and the hands of his two daughters, the LORD being merciful to *him*. . . ."

In spite of his bad choices and the chaos those choices brought upon him, Scripture testifies that Lot was a chosen child of God:

> [God,] turning the cities of Sodom and Gomorrah into ashes, condemned them to destruction, making them an example to those who afterward would live ungodly; and delivered righteous Lot, who was oppressed by the filthy conduct of the wicked (for that righteous man, dwelling among them, tormented his righteous soul from day to day by seeing and hear-

ing their lawless deeds)—then the Lord knows how to deliver the godly out of temptations and to reserve the unjust under punishment for the day of judgment. (2 Peter 2:6–9)

Lot and his wife left Sodom, but with great reluctance. As soon as they were out of the vicinity of Sodom, God rained down fire and brimstone on the land, leaving Sodom and Gomorrah in fiery ruins. No one dwelling in those cities that day survived God's judgment. Lot, his wife, and his two daughters escaped to the nearby city of Zoar. They had much to be thankful for. God had demonstrated his mercy. Lot's wife also had the presence of her husband and daughters for comfort. But in spite of God's provision and their safe haven in Zoar, Lot's wife had little room for gratitude in her worldly mind. Scripture tells us that she looked back and was turned into a pillar of salt (Gen. 19:26). It is not known for sure what phenomenon God used to miraculously destroy those wicked cities or precisely what is meant by "a pillar of salt." But whatever was meant, it was such that Moses, the author of Genesis, used poetic language, "a pillar of salt," to describe her fate.

Leap Before You Look

What are the implications that underlie such a backward look? Reflect for a moment on the family's escape. They had no time to pack necessary supplies, much less prized family treasures and other luxuries. They arrived safely in Zoar with only the clothes on their backs. The life that Lot's wife had known, likely since childhood, was gone. She found herself in the city of Zoar with nothing to commend her to a place of social status, no wealth, and no home. Her look back at Sodom, therefore, was no idle glance of curiosity; rather, it was a look of longing. Lot's wife left Sodom, but her heart never did. Perhaps her look back indicates that she physically ran back toward her former home in the burning city and got too close to the hail of fire. In either case, God allowed Lot's wife to go the way of her heart.

What about us? When we are awakened to the fact that we are living in the midst of pervasive sin, we too must often flee by whatever means God provides. If God in his mercy calls us to run, fleeing is our wisest course, no matter the personal cost. It is always safest and always best. God will see to it that we don't lose anything we truly need in the process. Jesus has promised,

> "Assuredly, I say to you, there is no one who has left house or brothers or sisters or father or mother or wife or children or lands, for My sake and the gospel's, who shall not receive a hundredfold now in this time—houses and brothers and sisters and mothers and children and lands, with persecutions— and in the age to come, eternal life." (Mark 10:29–30)

Now let's tie the story of Lot's wife to Angela, Amy, Madeline, and Lynn. Although Angela, Amy, and Madeline, unlike Lot's wife, profess faith in God, they are flirting with Sodom. They are dabbling in its pleasures, thinking they can have the safety God offers alongside the world.

Although there is no sin in Angela's love of fashion, or in the well-being she derives from physical fitness, or in pursuing a top position in her career, her lifestyle becomes sinful when it consumes her passion for the things of God. Her keen interest in Hollywood gossip may indicate a love of the world, and in light of eternity, perhaps a poor use of her time and mental energy.

What about Amy? If she continues to spend her free time dating godless men, she may never develop the spiritual capacity to enjoy men of faith, thus robbing herself of true companionship. God might intervene and, as he did with Lot's wife, lead her forcibly by the hand to safety, perhaps to a godly mate. However, if she is to enjoy God's best, she needs to cultivate her heart in the right direction now, lest she find herself dissatisfied with God's best later. That will likely happen if her heart lingers in the Sodom where she has dwelt for so long.

Who owns Madeline's heart? We cannot judge. She'll know, however, if her husband's wealth disappears and her social standing along with it. Would she find, then, renewed trust in God, who, unlike money, never fails? If her self-crafted identity were crushed, would she feel utterly lost? God, in his mercy, may test her this way.

Do you find yourself identifying with Angela or Amy or Madeline? Or do you have the joyous contentment of Lynn? The test will come when God sends something into your life that may necessitate your leaving cherished things behind. Will you go willingly, or will you linger in your compromise? If you linger, you will assuredly miss out on much great pleasure that God has for you, in this lifetime and for all eternity.

5

Rebekah

A Match Made in Heaven

Tick Tock

Most people get married at some point in their lives. That has been true throughout history. Yet in Western culture today, the number of marriages is declining, and people are marrying later in life. If you are a single Christian woman, perhaps you long to meet a mate, a companion with whom to live out your faith in day-to-day life.

A decade or two ago, women usually married right out of high school or college, settled down as homemakers, and were rearing children in their twenties. That has changed. Women are beginning families in their thirties and even forties. Some of these women settle down later by choice, often because they want to experience the success of a career first. In an age that advocates having it all, many women complete their education and go forward with a plan to enjoy independence for a decade or so before settling down to family life. That way they can look back and feel that they have not missed anything life has to offer.

But things do not work out so neatly in many cases. As many of these women enter their thirties, feeling lonely and sick of the corporate lifestyle, they are finding that the majority of their male counterparts are already married, and those who are not are directing their interest toward younger women. For the first time they feel the panic of the ticking biological clock.

On the flip side are those women who never cared much about developing a career. They desired marriage and family quite young but never met someone to love. These women develop careers out of necessity, waiting and hoping to meet Mr. Right. They too hear the clock, wondering if and how they will meet a suitable mate.

Christian women are no exception to this pattern of postponed marriage. As panic takes root and begins to clamor loudly enough, Christian women, like women everywhere, try to bring about a change to their single status in any number of ways. For women of faith, fervent prayer is surely included. Some also join a gym or get a new hairstyle in a renewed attempt to attract attention. Still others hop from church to church in order to meet as many single Christian men as possible. Many of these women are so swept up in their anxiety over the issue that they do not wait for God, or they refuse to submit to his will. They compromise by getting involved in relationships outside of biblical guidelines. What about you? If you are a single Christian woman, do you long to meet a man with whom you can share life within the intimacy of marriage? If so, are you handling your desire in a godly way?

Perhaps you are already married. If so, can you look back with thanksgiving for how God brought you and your spouse together? Or perhaps your marriage isn't all you had hoped for, and as you reflect on your courtship, you wonder now if you got ahead of God by your efforts to fulfill your desire. If that describes you, there is no need for despair. God is merciful. He knows we are weak. He has compassion on a woman's heart and understands our longing for love and family. If you moved ahead of God and you now wonder if you missed his best, rest assured that all is not lost. Not only does he work all things together for good; he can also bring great blessings out of your failures. Remember that even if you took yourself off of God's course, it is he who moved aside and allowed you to do so, and he also has plans to bring good out of your misjudgment or sin.

Whether married or single, we can learn a lot about God's sovereign care from Rebekah, another woman whose story is recounted in the book of Genesis. But before we look at Rebekah, think carefully about the following questions if you are contemplating marriage. The answers you give are crucial with regard to your walk with God and to your overall well-being. The first is this: If you are single and would like to be married, are you fully willing to submit to God's will for your life in this matter? Second, will you wait for his choice of a mate, even if it differs from your timetable? Finally, are you willing to remain single if that is how God has determined that you will bring the most glory to him? When you can answer "yes" to these questions, you are on the road to contentment and happiness, because God has ordained that true happiness is linked to living for him.

A Woman of Dependent Means

Rebekah is introduced in Scripture as a single woman. She came from a God-fearing family, so it is likely that prayer had been offered concerning Rebekah's future with a suitable mate. In the days when Rebekah lived, a woman was not free to gad about seeking a mate. Nor did she set aside Saturday nights for the enjoyment of male company. Dating just did not happen. In fact, dating as a means of courtship did not exist prior to the twentieth century. Rebekah lived with her parents in a God-centered home of some financial means. Although there were servants present in the home, there were certain household tasks that fell to her to do, and that is what she was doing when God came and changed her life. In one day her prayer was answered, a day that revealed the culmination of all God had done to bring about her heart's desire. It is exciting to realize that God is always working on our behalf in ways we cannot see at the time.

Some weeks before, in the land of Canaan, the patriarch Abraham decided that the time had come to find a wife for his precious son,

Isaac. Isaac was forty years old, certainly time for him to be starting a family of his own. Additionally, Abraham's beloved wife, Sarah, had recently died bringing great grief to the household. The timing was right for a new and joyful beginning. So Abraham sent his faithful servant out beyond the land of Canaan to find the right woman for Isaac along with a list of requirements that the right bride must meet. First and foremost, she must be a godly woman and one from among Abraham's people. She must also be willing to leave her family and everything about her previous life in order to return with the servant to settle with Isaac in Canaan.

Pledging to select a woman who fulfilled those criteria, the servant began his journey. As he traveled he was plagued with tension. Suppose he met several women who fit the bill? How would he know which one was God's choice? What if he met no one eligible? He so wanted to please his master, Abraham, that the thought of returning home with no bride for Isaac was devastating. So he wasted no time but traveled straight to Nahor, the city where Abraham's relatives lived, knowing that this was the most likely place to meet a woman who fit the criteria.

At evening time that first day in Nahor, the servant shrewdly placed himself beside the well outside of the city. It was a good place to begin his quest; the task of gathering water for the household always fell to the women, so he was sure to encounter them there. While he waited, the servant prayed. In fact, he prayed specifically. He asked that the first woman who would give him a drink of water, as well as offer to supply water for his camels, would be the chosen bride.

Before he had even finished praying, along came Rebekah with her water pitcher on her shoulder. Could she be the one? He approached her and asked for a drink, and his spirit soared when she offered to water his camels as well. In addition to her diligence, she was kind and generous, evidencing more traits of godly character. Then, upon discovering that this godly woman was the daughter of Abraham's people, the servant was so overjoyed that he gave her gifts of jewelry and asked to accompany her back to her home.

Most likely curious and excited as to the mission of this kindly man, Rebekah ran home to tell her father, who at once came back to the well to welcome the stranger from Canaan. Once inside their home, the servant poured out his story to the family, beginning with Abraham's requirements for a wife for his son and ending with how God had led him straight to Rebekah. Now, would she be willing to accompany him back to Canaan to be the wife of Isaac? Would she! Although she had never met Isaac, Rebekah was in no doubt that God had brought about his will for her in these circumstances, and she was most eager to go. God was showering blessing down upon her, for not only was Isaac the son of the patriarch Abraham; he was also well-established and able to provide her with a nice home.

The servant, eager to return to his master with God's gift, made preparations to leave with Rebekah the next morning, but Rebekah's parents balked when they saw him packing. *It's too soon*, they thought, and they tried to reason with the servant. *We need ten days with our daughter. We may never see her again.* But the servant was adamant. So they decided to leave the decision up to Rebekah. Would she leave that very day? She eagerly complied. God had made his will known; there was no reason to delay.

So Rebekah, along with her nursemaid, set out with Abraham's servant and the large caravan heading for Canaan. The pinnacle of God's great blessing happened at the end of their long journey: "Now Isaac came from the way of Beer Lahai Roi, for he dwelt in the South. And Isaac went out to meditate in the field in the evening; and he lifted his eyes and looked, and there, the camels were coming. Then Rebekah lifted her eyes, and when she saw Isaac she dismounted from her camel; for she had said to the servant, 'Who is this man walking in the field to meet us?' The servant said, 'It is my master.' So she took a veil and covered herself. And the servant told Isaac all the things that he had done. Then Isaac brought her into his mother Sarah's tent; and he took Rebekah and she became his wife, and he loved her. So Isaac was comforted after his mother's death" (Gen. 24:62–67).

In Capable Hands

What can we learn from Rebekah? Here was a woman who, based on the customs of that time, surely desired marriage. How did she go about making her dream come true? Her efforts were not extravagant or far-reaching or manipulative. We should not suppose that, prior to her encounter with the servant, Rebekah went about her business resigned to a fate of lonely spinsterhood. Rather, she would have entrusted her life and all her desires over into God's hands, assuredly through prayer, leaving all the details to him in a spirit of patience and submission. Then she would have gotten up and gone about living her day-to-day life as she had been doing before.

As we noted, women then had little opportunity to develop relationships with men outside their families. Yet, since suitable marriages benefited families, Rebekah would have her parents and others working on her behalf. Suitable mates were chosen by the parents, and both sets of parents had to be in agreement for a marriage to happen. So if a suitable single man had been presented to Rebekah and her family prior to now, she likely would have been married already. But God was preserving her for his choice.

Rebekah did not lie in bed, depressed over her single status. What was she doing when God brought her to marriage? She was going about her daily tasks. It was in the very process of performing a mundane chore that God came and changed her life. That should quell panic about staying home on Friday night, or working in an environment where Christian men are scarce, or belonging to a church that lacks a large singles scene. God has called each one of us to specific tasks in specific places at specific times in our lives. We don't have to change those or supplement them for fear of missing God's blessing. He brings his blessings to us, as long as we are living in obedience to his Word.

Freedom vs. Friday Night Futility

So many single women go home exhausted from work on a Friday evening, only to transform their appearance to go back out for a night of superficial socializing. How many of these evenings are spiritually rewarding, or even fun? If they are honest, women who do this will likely admit that these evenings are usually quite unrewarding. Why do they go then? It has less to do with the hope of meeting someone than it does with fear—fear that if they give in to their exhaustion and stay home, they will miss out on something.

There is a great blessing to be realized in the midst of such anxiety—something Jesus died to bring us—and that is freedom. We are free to stay home on the weekends. We are free to worship in the church where God has called us. We are free to give up the singles social dance in order to keep a long-standing dinner commitment with great-aunt Helen. We are free because Jesus purchased that freedom for us on the cross. We no longer have to work for our blessings. Instead, everything we need is now providentially supplied because Jesus earned our blessings for us.

We do, however, have to live in obedience to God's Word, which is what Rebekah was doing. One means of obedience is glorifying God in how we live each day. We are to work diligently and cheerfully at what he has placed before us to do. If we do this, even when doing so looks like a hindrance to something we hope for, we are living in submission to God, trusting that he is control. If we seek to please him in this way while we pursue godly character, he will take care of the rest. Again, it is not that we are earning his blessings; rather, he delights to honor the trust we place in him, and he does so by means of his many gifts, spiritual and temporal.

Contentment: A Choice

Rebekah's demeanor toward Abraham's servant indicates that she had a trusting and submissive spirit. Women who are angry with God, who are miserable without the thing they long for, are rarely able to be cheerful and industrious. Women who can relinquish their desires to God resemble Rebekah. They arrive at the well, ready for work and able to be generous to others in need. Women like that have learned a great secret: When we pray, leaving our longings in God's hands, asking him to conform our desires to his will, he will do so. That is the kind of prayer the outcome of which we can be confident. God will not leave us pining away—we do that to ourselves!

I have seen so many women who desire to be married compromise in their choice of a marriage partner, even when that partner is a Christian. As long as you marry another believer you do not sin; yet even among legitimate choices, there is always good, better, and best. The women who are surrendered to God's will in the matter of marriage are prone to hold out for the best. Fear, or lack of trust, or an insistence on getting our desire fulfilled in our way and timing can often lead us to make mediocre choices. Women who fall prey to bad decisions are the ones who frequently wind up married to spiritually immature men, or to men whose goals are aimed in an opposite direction from their own. When such marriages result, it is often because the woman has rationalized that since the potential spouse is a believer, everything will turn out all right in the end. In those cases sometimes it does; often it does not.

We have choices that women in other cultures and previous ages have never had. We are free to choose our marriage partners. Given that we live in an age where marriage is not necessary for survival, I am convinced that we should hold out for one that will, to the best of our knowledge, most enhance our relationship with God and the unique calling he has given us, and if such never comes along, we are best off remaining single.

The bottom line is this: If it is God's will for you to be married, it will happen. You are free to live for him. You don't have to spend your energy trying to help him get you married. When and if the time comes, you will know. God will see to it.

6

Rachel and Leah

Foul Play

It's Not Whether You Win or Lose, but . . .

What is it about sporting events that makes our adrenaline flow? Why do touchdowns, field goals, and three-point baskets propel us off the bleachers in raucous cheers? It is what we call team spirit, which is another name for good, old-fashioned rivalry. Rivalry like this is good-natured fun. God built into us a competitive spirit that, when rightly used, can be a great blessing. Good-natured rivalry can motivate us to all sorts of constructive activities and goals.

Sometimes, though, rivalry can take a sinful twist. When someone will do anything to win, to acquire a desirable end, no matter the cost personally and to others, good-natured competition has become a deadly contest. Many of us witnessed an example of that several years ago when Olympic skating hopeful Tonya Harding arranged to have her opponent's knee smashed with an iron bar.

We encounter less extreme examples every day: teenage girls competing for the attention of a handsome boy; advertising campaigns of public officials vying for office; siblings in competition for parental love and approval. Perhaps the most common of all such competitions, sibling rivalry, does not occur only within nuclear families. It also occurs in the family of God. Sinful rivalry can and does spring up all too easily among Christian brothers and sisters.

Rivalry of this type is a violation of the Tenth Commandment, which states, "You shall not covet your neighbor's house; you shall not covet your neighbor's wife, nor his male servant, nor his female servant, nor his ox, nor his donkey, nor anything that is your neighbor's" (Exod. 20:17). Rivalry of the sort we are talking about is covetousness. It may be defined as the inordinate desire to possess something or someone at any cost. It is lust. Sometimes it simmers quietly; at other times it rages openly; and to varying degrees, we are all guilty. What sort of things can hook us into sinful rivalry? The object of lust like this can be material. Some people will sacrifice all their free hours, time with those they love, even their health, in order to acquire a bigger house, a better car, or more luxurious vacations. Sometimes lust sets in for intangible things like reputation, power, or seeking to be admired. Other times a person is the focus of covetous rivalry.

How You Play the Game

We see this sort of covetousness woven into a story in Genesis. It is a story about two sisters named Rachel and Leah. Their rivalry stretched out over many years, as can be seen from reading about it in Genesis 29–33. It all started because a man named Jacob, son of Isaac and Rebekah, wandered into their lives one day and fell instantly in love with Rachel. So enthralled was Jacob with the beautiful Rachel that he agreed to tend her father's sheep for seven years in order to marry her. "So Jacob served seven years for Rachel, and they seemed only a few days to him because of his love for her" (Gen. 29:20).

Leah, however, was devastated by this chain of events. Onto the scene had come this eligible man who had eyes only for Rachel; this was doubly painful, no doubt, since Leah was the older of the two and, thus, had assuredly hoped that she would be the first one married, as was the custom of the day. From the story we are also given the idea that Leah did not possess the physical assets with which Rachel had been endowed. We are told, "Now Laban had two daughters: the name of the elder was Leah, and the name of the younger was Rachel. Leah's eyes were delicate, but Rachel was beautiful of form and appearance" (Gen. 29:16–17). We do not know for sure what was wrong with Leah's eyes, but from the way the verse is structured to make a comparison, we can assume that, whatever it was, the flaw detracted from her appearance.

The elements for sibling rivalry were in place even before Jacob arrived: two sisters of marriageable age, both desirous of a husband. Due to her status as eldest sister, Leah was more eligible for Jacob, yet Rachel was the possessor of great beauty, surely a desirable trait in a wife. All it took was a single man seeking a mate to trigger trouble in this family, which is what happened when Jacob appeared. If he had fallen in love with Leah, the rivalry would not, most likely, have gotten off the ground. Since custom dictated that the elder should marry first, Rachel would have accepted the situation. But that is not what happened, and as the story tells us, Jacob's feelings for the younger Rachel stirred up passionate competition between the two sisters.

The father of the two girls, Laban, had devised a secret scheme that would solve the dilemma, or so he thought. It was a scheme that came to light just after Jacob and Rachel were to have been married. Jacob had served his seven years tending Laban's sheep, so the time to marry Rachel arrived. In those days a marriage was celebrated by means of a large feast, after which the bride was given to the groom, and the couple would slip off into the privacy of a tent to consummate the marriage. All went according to plan, and Jacob took his veiled bride away and spent the night with her. But Laban's trick had worked. When morning light dawned, Jacob discovered that it was not Rachel lying beside him—it was Leah!

What had happened? Laban had slyly hidden Leah beneath the bridal veil, and in the darkness, Jacob had not known the difference. In shock Jacob confronted Laban and asked, "What is this you have done to me? Was it not for Rachel that I served you? Why then have you deceived me?" And Laban said, "It must not be done so in our country, to give the younger before the firstborn" (Gen. 29:25–26).

So Laban struck another deal with Jacob by offering him Rachel also, on the condition that he would serve another seven years. This time, however, not wanting to test Jacob's limits too strongly, Laban promised Jacob he could have Rachel one week hence, prior to serving out the additional years of farmwork. Laban was devious. Not only was he getting a good husband for both daughters; he also managed to manipulate fourteen years of labor from this devoted man. Perhaps Laban was sick to death of dealing with the quarrels between his daughters. If so, his plot held out hope for a return to peace in the household.

A couple of mysteries still remain as to that fateful wedding day. First, where was Rachel when Jacob slipped off with Leah? The story doesn't tell us. Was she brought into the plot with her father, confident that Jacob loved her enough to agree to Laban's underhanded terms? So confident that even if he married Leah too, he would love Rachel best? We hope not, because going along with the plot would indicate a lack of real love for her husband-to-be. Perhaps Rachel was forcibly restrained, hidden away out of sight all day while Jacob was tricked.

Whatever the case with Rachel, we know that Leah went along with the plot, most likely with great eagerness. Laban may have cajoled her to do it, but more likely, since she wanted Jacob for herself, she saw this as her only opportunity to get him. But whatever it was that drove her to participate in the deceptive marriage, she proceeded willingly. All night in the marriage tent she played along, knowing that Jacob believed that she was Rachel. The deceptive marriage was merely an indicator of the sisters' rivalry, one that had characterized the household since Jacob's arrival seven years earlier.

At the end of this tumultuous week, neither sister was the winner. Rachel's wedded bliss was marred by having to share her new husband with another woman, and Leah knew that Jacob had been tricked into marrying her and that his real love was reserved for

Rachel. So, far from being over, even stiffer competition had been set up between the sisters.

Sudden-Death Overtime

As Jacob fulfilled his promise to Laban over the next seven years, the Genesis story focuses on the intense conflict between Rachel and Leah. As we read the narrative, we almost feel like spectators at a competitive sporting event, but this game was far from harmless because the pawns were human beings. As we learned when we studied the life of Jacob's grandmother, Sarah, bearing children was crucial for the social survival of women in the ancient Near East. Children, especially sons, ensured a woman a place of respect in the community, as well as material provision for old age. Barrenness was a social stigma, whereas a woman who produced sons earned respect. It was this issue that fueled the flames of rivalry between Rachel and Leah.

Leah bore four sons in rapid succession, while Rachel produced none. The way the story is recounted in Genesis gives us an idea of the marital tension that characterized the household:

> When the LORD saw that Leah was unloved, He opened her womb; but Rachel was barren. So Leah conceived and bore a son, and she called his name Reuben; for she said, "The LORD has surely looked on my affliction. Now therefore, my husband will love me." Then she conceived again and bore a son, and said, "Because the LORD has heard that I am unloved, He has therefore given me this son also." And she called his name Simeon. She conceived again and bore a son, and said, "Now this time my husband will become attached to me, because I have borne him three sons." Therefore his name was called Levi. And she conceived again and bore a son, and said, "Now I will praise the LORD." Therefore she called his name Judah. Then she stopped bearing. (Gen. 29:31–35)

It is obvious that, above all other considerations, Leah was grasp-
ing for her husband's love. But do you see how her attempts to win
him through childbearing failed to bring her what she wished? Leah
was discovering what we all must, namely, that relying on our
strengths, special blessings, or superior abilities will not bring us what
we hope for. Only God can do that. Producing sons for Jacob failed
to bring Leah the love she craved, but not until her fourth son was
born did she begin to realize that. Finally, at the birth of Judah, she
was beginning to understand. Her focus had become more God-centered, as we see from her words at his birth: "Now I will praise the
Lord," she said. It is interesting, too, that it was this son, Judah, from
whom Jesus Christ was descended.

Our Compassionate Coach

God hates our rivalries! He knows how unnecessary and fruitless
they are and how they consume our lives. We do not have to spend
our energies competing with others for what we want. If it is something or someone God wants us to have, he will provide it. Look at
his care for Leah, his understanding of her woman's heart, in Genesis 29:31: "When the LORD saw that Leah was unloved, He opened
her womb." In spite of Leah's trickery, her attempts to steal Jacob's
affection from Rachel, God was determined to bless her. But his blessing for her was different from the blessing he had provided for Rachel.
Jacob's love was God's provision for Rachel, so that meant that he
had something else in store for Leah. In trying to steal someone else's
blessing, Leah was thwarted in the thing for which she lusted.

But regardless of that, God had great compassion on Leah. He
knows and understands the heart of a woman, the passionate desire
to be loved. So although God was not about to give Rachel's gift to
Leah, he nevertheless provided her with Jacob's favor by means of a
fruitful womb. God also provided her with the love for which she
yearned through the children she bore, if only she would look there
for it.

What do you imagine Rachel was feeling through the successive births of Leah's sons? Rachel knew that Jacob loved her, yet because Leah was fertile he likely spent many a night in Leah's tent, leaving Rachel lonely and jealous. So Rachel sought to acquire the blessing God had given to Leah. Rachel was no longer satisfied with merely the love of her husband; she wasn't about to let Leah take on the role of family matriarch. After Judah's birth, Rachel and Jacob had an argument.

"Now when Rachel saw that she bore Jacob no children, Rachel envied her sister, and said to Jacob, 'Give me children, or else I die!' And Jacob's anger was aroused against Rachel, and he said, 'Am I in the place of God, who has withheld from you the fruit of the womb?' " (Gen. 30:1–2). What fueled the intensity of Rachel's yearning for off-spring, a desire so intense that she preferred death to barrenness? In this case, it was much more than societal pressure; it was the lust to possess what her sister had been given. Her role as prized wife was no longer satisfying to Rachel. That is because once covetousness has become an obsession, we tend to lose sight of our blessings.

Shortly after Rachel's argument with her husband, the rivalry took on the intensity of a sudden-death playoff or an overtime inning. Rachel did bear two sons to Jacob and two more by means of her ser-vant, just as Sarah had attempted to do with her maid Hagar. Not to be outdone, Leah provided Jacob with two sons from her maid, as well as two more from her own body. When the competition was over, Jacob had fathered twelve sons through four different women.

And the Winner Is . . .

Time passed, and the additional seven years of labor promised to Laban were completed. The family prepared to move back to Jacob's homeland, a family grown large but nevertheless worn down and bat-tle-weary. The seven years had been harsh ones for Rachel and Leah as their energies were consumed in outdoing each other. Where did all the striving get them? After bearing Jacob six sons, did Leah come

out with an equal share of his heart? And what about Rachel? Had
she borne enough children to secure a favored place in the family?
The answers are revealed as the family traveled back toward Jacob's
homeland.

Jacob was nervous about heading home because he feared an
encounter with his brother, Esau. Years before, Jacob had tricked Esau
out of his inheritance and had fled from home to avoid his brother's
justifiable wrath. Now, as Jacob drew near to home, he prepared himself for a hostile confrontation with Esau, and what he did to protect
himself shows us that Leah did not get what she had fought so hard
to win: "Now Jacob lifted his eyes and looked, and there, Esau was
coming, and with him were four hundred men. So he divided the children among Leah, Rachel, and the two maidservants. And he put the
maidservants and their children in front, Leah and her children
behind, and Rachel and Joseph [Rachel's son] last" (Gen. 33:1–2).
Obviously, in spite of Leah's having borne six of Jacob's twelve sons,
Jacob's affections had not changed. He placed Leah and her children
closer to the danger, while safeguarding Rachel and her offspring near
himself.

But that does not mean that Rachel had won. She had retained
her husband's love, God's gift to her. But she could not have Leah's
gift—a fruitful womb—in spite of her numerous attempts to get it.
The story tells us that, as the large caravan continued on its way to
Jacob's homeland,

> Then they journeyed from Bethel. And when there was but
> a little distance to go to Ephrath, Rachel labored in child-
> birth, and she had hard labor. Now it came to pass, when she
> was in hard labor, that the midwife said to her, "Do not fear;
> you will have this son also." And so it was, as her soul was
> departing (for she died), that she called his name Ben-Oni
> [son of my sorrow]; but his father called him Benjamin. So
> Rachel died and was buried on the way to Ephrath (that is,

Bethlehem). And Jacob set a pillar on her grave, which is the pillar of Rachel's grave to this day. (Gen. 35:16–20)

A waste of years. Energies, talents, and gifts frittered away and lost. Affection, however scanty, between two sisters destroyed. Are you bound up into a rivalry like that of Rachel and Leah? If so, I can say with surety that it is robbing you of much joy. Maybe an attractive single man has arrived on your church singles' scene, and you find yourself, along with many other women, seeking his attention. Are you manipulating circumstances to outdo your competitors? If so, you are wasting your time and energy. If God has purposed to give him to you, no one else will get him. Contrarily, God will not give you what he intends for another.

Or perhaps you find yourself in a competitive situation at work. That happened at one of my jobs. A woman was hired who shortly thereafter sought to take over, attempting to steal tasks from others that she wanted to do. I regret to say that I exhausted myself with anger and in trying to hold her at bay. I regained peace only when I let go and stopped competing with her and instead focused on the tasks that lay directly on my own desk. It was as if God were saying, "What does it matter what she takes from you? Are you here to serve yourself or me?" Once I got my focus off of myself and onto God's purposes, I was able to regain joy at my job.

Sometimes these rivalries are lifelong, especially in family situations. You might be someone who can identify with that. Maybe you have a sibling with a long-standing history of success, one with good grades in every subject, varsity letters in high school, popular, attractive, and self-assured from childhood forward. Children so gifted often receive well-deserved and constant praise for their achievements, yet this can leave a less successful sibling feeling inferior. Even well-meaning parents can deepen the rivalry between their children by setting the standards for all their offspring by the one who excels. This can traumatize children and teenagers well into adulthood and, short of God's grace, can take a lifetime to overcome.

The same applies to women who long for children yet cannot have them. A woman in that situation will not find happiness in interfering with someone else's children or in subtly attempting to steal their affection. If God has withheld children from you, ask God to fill that void with the means of his choosing. A woman I know discovered in her thirties that she would never bear children, and a friend directed her to Isaiah 54:

> "Sing, O barren,
> You who have not borne!
> Break forth into singing, and cry aloud,
> You who have not labored with child!
> For more are the children of the desolate
> Than the children of the married woman," says the LORD.
> (Isa. 54:1)

Although in the original context Isaiah was prophesying about the return of the Israelites from exile, the lesson from God is for you and me as well. If he withholds children from you, he does not intend to leave your life empty; rather, he has other plans of blessing to occupy that empty place.

Perhaps you are a woman who grew up in the shadow of a superlative sibling, and you doubt your ability to accomplish anything. If so, do not waste your life trying to measure up, to accomplish the same things as that brother or sister, or to live for parental praise. Instead, seek your unique gifts from God. He has created you with them and calls you to live them out. Your specialness will shine as you discover them and put them into practice.

Time Out!

If you can identify with any of these situations or others like them, what have you been doing about it? There is only one thing to do, something we learn from the tragic rivalry between Rachel and Leah.

The key lies in discovering your unique gifts and blessings from God and focusing your energies on those. Do not waste time in trying to fulfill your desire by competing with others.

One of the main considerations to keep in mind in putting to death a sinfully competitive heart is how such sin grieves God. His word tells us to count others better than ourselves, to look out for the interests of others (Phil. 2:4). He commands us not to lust after what belongs to someone else (Exod. 20:17). He promises to supply all of our needs in Christ Jesus (Phil. 4:19). When we compete with our sisters in Christ, when we allow ourselves to get sucked into ungodly rivalries with anyone, the love of Christ is diminished from our witness.

If there is something or someone you want but do not have, pray about it. Then thank God for your life as it is now. As you do, you'll discover a new sense of purpose and abundant joy in life just as it is today.

7

Dinah

The Boredom Blues

Wander Lust

"Another Saturday night with nothing to do," lamented Katy. As she pondered possible alternatives, Katy remembered something she had heard at work about a new club on Delaware Avenue. Her co-workers were talking about it at lunch this week, how much fun they'd had there dancing and mingling with the after-work crowd. Katy debated whether this new place could provide a solution to an otherwise empty evening, and as dusk approached the thought became more and more appealing. Laughter, music, and numerous people to talk to. Maybe she would even meet someone special.

The idea of going there alone was a bit intimidating, so Katy considered which of her friends might be available at the last minute. No one from church. They probably wouldn't have an interest in a place like this. Most of the women in her congregation preferred more sedate evenings. She remembered also that the church was hosting a social event this evening, and most of the women she knew would be attending that anyway. Going to the church social did not appeal to Katy. She was bored with that crowd; what they considered to be fun, Katy found rather dull. Just the same old people. So Katy called Erin, one of the co-workers who had mentioned the new club.

As she drove with Erin to Delaware Avenue, Katy was glad to have something to do. They paid the cover charge for admittance, and as they entered, they were immediately enveloped in a haze of smoke and loud music. It truly was exciting, just as the others had said. It was hard to see in the dim lighting, but Katy made out clusters of people, many of them attractive men. Well, after another drink, Katy decided, she would make her way toward the dance floor.

As she stood near the bar talking with Erin, two men approached to engage them in conversation. One of them was very attractive, Katy thought as she bantered with him. Flirting was harmless and a lot of fun. His name was Ken, and he asked her to dance.

Much later Katy realized that she had not seen Erin for several hours. She and Ken (she didn't know his last name) had been dancing all evening. Had Erin gone home? Was she somewhere else on the dance floor? Katy gave it only a passing thought. She was having fun with Ken, and Erin was sophisticated enough to take care of herself, she thought. Eventually Ken suggested that the two of them leave the club and go somewhere to talk. Katy felt comfortable with Ken and found his attentiveness exhilarating, so she readily agreed. The thought of going home to her empty apartment dulled any qualms about going somewhere alone with a man she'd just met.

Ken had suggested a quiet coffee house in midtown where they could sit and get to know each other, and they made small talk as he drove through the streets of the city. In the back of Katy's mind, she knew she should be thinking about going home. She had to get up for church in the morning, and it was past midnight, but she was reluctant to leave. She could tell Ken was attracted to her. Was he a man she could really like? Was he a Christian? Well, she wouldn't think about that tonight. Time enough for that tomorrow. Right now she would enjoy the fact that this attractive man wanted to spend time with her. Eventually Ken pulled into the empty parking lot behind a darkened restaurant. "It's closed," Katy pointed out. But Ken pulled into a secluded space and turned off the ignition.

"We can talk right here then. I had a few drinks, and I probably shouldn't drive any more just now," he replied.

Within Katy began the first tingling of nervousness. "Oh, I can walk home from here," she said, trying to sound casual. But as she unhooked her seatbelt and gathered her coat and purse, Ken reached out and pulled her toward him.

"Hey," he said, "we danced together all evening. Just relax for awhile. You can't leave me like this."

"No, I really have to go," she insisted, struggling to get out from under his embrace. "Not yet you don't," Ken insisted, his face turning ugly. Panicking, Katy turned the door handle and jumped out of the car.

"Fine then!" Ken yelled, starting the ignition. "You can find your own way home!"

He roared out of the parking lot, leaving Katy alone and isolated. Shaking, she hurried toward the well-lit street, realized that she had left her new coat in his car. She hurried toward home, unable to hail a cab, having exhausted her cash supply at the club. "God," she prayed, "please get me home safely! I know this was a stupid thing to do. If I had gone to the church social, I'd be home safe and asleep this very moment. I've just been so bored and wanted some excitement. But this is way more than I bargained for!"

Does Katy's story shock you? Most likely not, because we hear about such folly occurring in every city in the Western world every Saturday night. Christian women are not excluded. Perhaps you know firsthand what I am talking about. This is nothing new to our era, either. It has happened throughout history, even in Bible times. It happened to Dinah, the daughter of Leah and Jacob, and the results then were like they are today—defiling, humiliating, and destructive.

Stop!

Jacob and his large family had settled near Shechem, a Canaanite city. The people of the community were pagans, worshiping idols and living for worldly pleasure. Quite naturally, Dinah and her eleven brothers would have become acquainted with their neighbors. The Canaanite lifestyle probably seemed glamorous and exciting to the young woman compared with her home life. Dinah's mother, Leah, was too caught up in her rivalry with Rachel to give her daughter the attention and guidance a young woman needs from her mother, and her brothers likely spent the majority of their time with one another sharing mutual male interests, thus leaving Dinah with little companionship.

So it is not surprising when we read in Genesis that Dinah ventured out one day to spend time with "the daughters of the land" (Gen. 34:1). The Canaanite women, not being constrained by considerations of godliness, took liberties that were prohibited to women from families like Dinah's. To a lonely, bored young woman, the worldliness of the Canaanites held great allure. And the young men! Cultured and sophisticated! So when Shechem, the Hivite prince of the region, paid Dinah attention, she was flattered, but subsequently she found herself in dire circumstances. The story tells us, "When Shechem the son of Hamor the Hivite, prince of the country, saw her, he took her and lay with her, and violated her" (Gen. 34:2).

Just as Katy had done, Dinah placed herself in a setting that left her vulnerable. In Dinah's case, however, she lost more than a new coat. What happened to Dinah is today termed date rape. Although no man has the right ever, at any time, to take from a woman what she is not willing to give, the fact remains that when date rape occurs, a woman has first placed herself in a situation where the act can happen. That means that many of these cases could be avoided if a little prudence were to be exercised ahead of time.

As far as Prince Shechem was concerned, this was no casual encounter. He loved Dinah, so he sent his father, Hamor, to ask for her hand in marriage. But back on Jacob's dwelling, her brothers were infuriated over Dinah's defilement. Some of her older brothers vowed to take revenge, and they devised a plot. They told Hamor they would agree to let Shechem marry their younger sister if all the males in the city would first pledge allegiance to Jehovah by undergoing the covenant rite of circumcision. Hamor, in seeking to provide his son with the woman he desired, and believing an alliance with the family of Jacob would be beneficial to his small kingdom, agreed to the terms. So off Dinah went to the home of Shechem to be his wife.

But three days later, when all the men of Shechem were weakened from the pain of circumcision, Jacob's sons Simeon and Levi rushed into the city and killed every man within its gates, including Shechem and his father, Hamor. Jacob was greatly distressed. He said to Simeon and Levi, " 'You have troubled me by making me obnoxious among the inhabitants of the land, among the Canaanites and the Perizzites; and since I am few in number, they will gather themselves together against me and kill me. I shall be destroyed, my household and I.' But they said, 'Should he treat our sister like a harlot?' " (Gen. 34:30–31).

In Dinah's case the consequences were much worse than Katy's. Shechem's sexual sin robbed Dinah of her purity, something that could never be regained. In addition to the shameful stigma she would carry, great destruction came about as a result. The reputation of Jacob's family was ruined, and the men of Shechem were dead.

Warning Signs for Wanderers

Can you relate to what we are talking about? Perhaps you have had an experience like Katy's, or even like Dinah's. If so, I am sure you suffered, if not physically, at least emotionally and spiritually, and you want to prevent another similar incident. We can learn from Dinah's story a great deal about how to avoid the consequences that can happen if we wander outside of God's path.

What stirs us to seek meaningful companionship outside of other believers? For some it is the feeling of rejection by the Christian community because of baggage from their past. Divorced Christians often feel this way. In other cases, women in the throes of a struggle with a besetting sin find themselves afraid to open up in a Christian setting. They think, "If others really knew me, they'd want nothing to do with me." That sort of fear and insecurity leaves them feeling isolated from the people who could offer encouragement.

Others live largely in a worldly environment so, for them, such company feels more like home. Women with careers requiring regular business travel are prone to that because they are left with little or no Christian companionship week after week. Or perhaps, since becoming a Christian, you have never really turned back from the world and its allure. You find yourself bored with Christian people and activities, and you long for greater stimulation. Maybe you have grown weary of waiting for God to provide a companion or a group of friends, and a spirit of impatience has set in. Or maybe you are so hungry for unconditional love that you'll look for it in all the wrong places.

These are some of the underlying feelings and thoughts that can throw wood on temptation's fire. The key is recognizing them as they assail you. If you are successful in identifying the source of your temptation, you can deal with it before it festers long enough to lead you into danger. Once you have identified what lies behind your desire for ungodly companionship, talk to God about it. You can be honest with him about your loneliness, your feelings of rejection, your insecurity. He cares about your pain. Tell him if you are struggling to let the world go. He wants to deepen your desire for godly companionship.

Careful Company

The people and situations to which we expose ourselves also play a key role in determining our desire to wander off godly paths. When we watch television indiscriminately, we are frequently feasting our eyes on sensual worldliness. When we spend a lot of off-work hours with our unregenerate co-workers, that is, those who are unbelievers, we will begin to desire what they desire and find that our thinking is being shaped by theirs. Paul wrote, "Do not be deceived: 'Evil company corrupts good habits' " (1 Cor. 15:33).

Our thought life also plays a key factor in determining our desires and actions. We downplay the role of fantasy. After all, we are tempted to rationalize, "It's not as if I'm doing those things I fantasize about." But the truth is, if we roll a sensuous thought over and over in our minds, it is much easier to go out and do it. Most of the big sins we fall into are the results of unwise choices and an accumulation of lesser sins over a long period of time.

Maybe you are a woman with a teenage daughter, and you worry that she might get into trouble like Dinah did. Mothers with teens in our society live in fear of the gut wrench that accompanies the mumbled, tearful confession, "I'm pregnant." Good mothers, Christian or not, apply careful attention to their daughters' activities and monitor their whereabouts. But sometimes, no amount of safeguarding prevents the horror of teenage pregnancy, date rape, or sexually transmitted disease. Do you have a daughter whom you sense might wander outside the safety of the limitations you have set? If so, ask yourself, is she content in her home? Are you providing a godly environment and setting a biblical example? Are you monitoring how she spends her time even during the hours she spends at home? Does she have an opportunity to spend time with other Christian young people on a weekly basis? If you have a teenager in trouble or one whom you fear is heading that way, perhaps there is something or someone being allowed in your home that is driving your daughter out the door.

As we have seen, that was true in Dinah's case. Her parents were hardly models of holy behavior. Her mother was consumed with outdoing her rival, Rachel. Her father, Jacob, gave his approval on Dinah's marriage to an unbeliever, indicating his lack of concern for her spiritual well-being. In fact, throughout Dinah's ordeal in Genesis 34, God is not mentioned one time. However, Dinah surely did not lack for love. On the basis of her brothers' reaction to Shechem's shameful treatment of her, she was assuredly loved and cherished by them, familial pride notwithstanding. There were likely a number of

factors that led Dinah to venture away from the safety of home, including her own sin.

Holy Boundaries

All of that leaves us asking, How do we deal with the inner turmoil that compels us toward trouble? The first thing to realize is that
God has his provision for our longings. We can confidently ask him
to take away our loneliness, trusting that he delights to answer this
prayer in the best way and in the perfect time. He will provide you
with fulfilling Christian companionship, and if it seems to be withheld for a season, it is only so that he can provide it to you directly
through himself.

There are also some things *you* can do to find the contentment God
has for you, and they begin with an acceptance of the circumstances
into which God has set your life. When God parceled off portions of
the Promised Land to the twelve tribes of Israel (Josh. 15–17), he drew
the boundary lines for each tribe based on his long-term plans for every
individual member of each tribe, as well as for his own glory. Just so,
he also draws boundary lines around our lives, and it is within those
parameters that we are free to live. The lines are drawn the same way
for every believer in terms of the ordinances laid forth in Scripture,
but in other ways they may vary. God's boundaries for you can be discovered when you consider your material circumstances, your gifts and
talents, your marital status and family, and the things that tempt you
to sin. We, as Christian women, have a responsibility to determine
where our boundary lines are drawn. The boundaries God establishes
for us can and will frequently shift at different points in our lives, either
widening or narrowing the arena where we are to live and serve him.[1]

When we stray outside the protectiveness of those lines, we set
ourselves up for unhappiness. Straying can occur when we focus our
attention on the world and what it offers. We begin to crave worldly
pleasures because we are not in tune with the abundant provision
God has for us where he has placed us. When we allow ungodly influ-

ences into our hearts and homes, sooner or later we will be conformed to that. Remember that it is sickness that is contagious, not health!

It is always and only within the particular boundaries God has drawn for each of his children that real happiness can be found. Look around you at what you have. Stop looking at what you don't have. Joy and fulfillment are available for you now! You have, I hope, discovered this for yourself. It is the way to truly live out the abundant life God has promised his people.

Back on Track

If you are a woman who has wandered off course, perhaps you are wondering how to get back within God's framework for your life. Ask him, and he will help you. He doesn't want you to miss his best. Read the parable of the prodigal son in Luke 15 for encouragement. Dinah's life was not over after she wandered. We do not read about her again, but we know that she returned to where she belonged, into a family set apart by God to live in a covenant relationship with himself, one set apart to receive all the blessings that are found by those who live within the covenant boundaries.

If you are far away today, these words from the prophet Joel hold out the promise waiting for you back home:

> "So I will restore to you the years that the swarming locust
> has eaten,
> The crawling locust,
> The consuming locust,
> And the chewing locust,
> My great army which I sent among you.
> You shall eat in plenty and be satisfied,
> And praise the name of the LORD your God,
> Who has dealt wondrously with you;
> And My people shall never be put to shame." (Joel 2:25–26)

8

Miriam

What about *Me?*

Whatever It Takes

When the history books are written, how will Hillary Clinton be remembered? Will it be the fortitude she showed in standing by her husband while his marital infidelities were paraded before the world? Will it be her successful bid for a New York Senate seat? Probably not. Hillary Clinton will likely be remembered as the woman who would do anything to come out on top.

In today's culture, this is lauded as the highest good a woman can achieve. Feminine graciousness, kindness, contentment, and patience are mere gloss on the hard wood of individual accomplishment, luxuries for women who have already arrived. They are no longer virtues to be cultivated. On the contrary, they should be cast aside if they interfere with personal success. What about a woman whose calling is centered in the home, pouring her energies on family members so that *they* can go forward and achieve success? Hillary Clinton expressed contempt for women who adopt that lifestyle, perhaps in an attempt to validate some of her choices along the way.

Clinton has worked hard to reach her goals. She has held and continues to hold a position of power, authority, and influence. Her every
move is written down and photographed. She is at the top by today's
standards. What Hillary Clinton has not yet realized is that true greatness, genuine success, and personal fulfillment are not found in any
sort of lasting way by doing whatever it takes to come out on top.

Beginning with the book of Exodus, we meet a woman who had
gifts and talents similar to Hillary Clinton's. Her name is Miriam, and
like Hillary, she had courage, intelligence, and tremendous leadership skills.

The Weakness of Personal Strength

The Bible weaves Miriam onto its pages several times at differing
stages of her life. We first read about her as a young girl whose task
was watching over her baby brother, an infant hidden away to escape
death in the bulrushes of the Nile River. It is there in Exodus 2 where
we first discover that Miriam was clever and courageous. When
Pharaoh's daughter stumbled upon the baby Moses and took him
home to rear, it was Miriam, the daughter of despised Hebrew slaves,
who boldly stepped forth and offered to find a nursemaid to breast-
feed Moses. Pharaoh's daughter accepted Miriam's offer, so Miriam
went and fetched their very own mother for the job. Thus, mother
and son were reunited and the baby boy was out of harm's way, all
because of the quick thinking of young Miriam.

We later hear of Miriam after the Israelites had miraculously crossed
the Red Sea, leaving the pursuing Egyptians behind to drown in a
thundering cascade of water. We read, "Then Miriam the prophet-
ess, the sister of Aaron, took the timbrel in her hand; and all the
women went out after her with timbrels and with dances. And Miriam
answered them,

> Sing to the LORD,
> For He has triumphed gloriously!

The horse and its rider
He has thrown into the sea! (Exod. 15:20–21)

It is evident that Miriam was a woman with high motivational skills, able to encourage others during hard times and to keep them focused on God.

As a result, Miriam had become one of the leading figures in the fast-growing tribe. Her leadership role may be attributed to a number of additional factors. Being the sister of Moses surely brought her a measure of status, but without her natural gifts the family connection would have been insufficient. What lent authority to Miriam within the tribe was her strong faith in God; during such a perilous time in Israelite history, such faith would have brought encouragement to the entire tribe.

It is not until further on in the story that we discover a character flaw in Miriam. The Israelites had been wandering in the wilderness for some time under the leadership of Moses. Moses had taken a new wife, an Ethiopian, or Cushite, woman. Moses' first wife, Zipporah, had likely died; either that or the Ethiopian woman was an additional wife. It was just after Moses' second marriage that Miriam spoke out critically against her brother and his new wife. We read, "Then Miriam and Aaron spoke against Moses because of the Ethiopian woman whom he had married; for he had married an Ethiopian woman. So they said, 'Has the LORD indeed spoken only through Moses? Has He not spoken through us also?' And the LORD heard it" (Num. 12:1–2).

At first glance, Miriam's criticism seems disconnected from Moses' new marriage. What had provoked her? Was it the new wife or the fact that Moses was God's appointed spokesman? Perhaps it was a misguided zeal to keep the tribe undefiled from outsiders, which the Ethiopians were at that time. Or maybe it was that Moses, her younger brother, was marrying for the second time, while she had not yet had one husband. Josephus, the ancient historian, recounts that Miriam did marry, but Scripture never mentions it. Another possibility is that

Miriam was upset because she, as older sister, a proven leader in her own right, was relegated to a lesser position of authority than her younger brother.

We can arrive at a probable answer if we think for a moment about Miriam's perspective. She had taken care of Moses since his infancy, all while enduring the intolerable conditions imposed upon the Hebrew slaves in Egypt. Then, after God brought the whole tribe safely away from Pharaoh and his pursuing army, Miriam had led the women in musical praise and thanksgiving to God for his miraculous deliverance. She had likely been a significant influence for good on the tribe, most especially the women, as they faced tedious days in the desert. Miriam was probably a woman of ceaseless energy, a true multitasker. If Moses' first wife, Zipporah, had died of an illness, Miriam would likely have been intensely involved in providing nursing care for the sick woman and overseeing domestic tasks. As Moses' sister, she would have been a logical caregiver in such a situation.

If Zipporah had indeed died, in all likelihood, it would have been Miriam who stepped in to console her brother and continue caring for his day-to-day needs. Then along came the new Ethiopian wife to reclaim the position of Moses' caretaker, relegating Miriam back to the sidelines in the process. It appears that Miriam greatly resented the intrusion into what she considered her territory on a number of fronts, and not the least of which was the intrusion of this woman from outside their special covenant community. It is no surprise that resentment began to simmer within Miriam.

If we are honest, we must admit that we respond like Miriam in such matters. At times like that, when we are feeling humiliated, mistreated, or used, a critical spirit is easily fostered within our hearts. Do you recognize that in yourself? Think about the times when you have lashed out at others. Is it not often because your ego has been injured? However, our pride prevents us from acknowledging that fact, either to ourselves or to others. Instead, we often cling to a spirit of self-righteous anger, all the while seeking a peripheral reason to justify our sinful emotions.

Miriam felt not only mistreated by her brother, but also her words seem to indicate that underneath she likely felt mistreated by God. Why had he appointed her brother as the leader? A man who would stoop to marrying an outsider! It wasn't fair! Hadn't she exhibited her capabilities? In her anger and simmering sense of injustice, she rationalized that she, being equally fit for the job, if not even more so, had just as much right to speak on God's behalf as Moses did. So, feeling thwarted, unappreciated, and undervalued, Miriam gave voice to these thoughts, as we are so often tempted to do. We can picture her whirling from person to person, dragging Aaron with her throughout the camp, voicing her complaints and trying to rally the tribe to her viewpoint.

That's Not Fair!

God, however, was very displeased with the incident. Afterward, we read, "So the anger of the LORD was aroused against them, and He departed. And when the cloud departed from above the tabernacle, suddenly Miriam became leprous, as white as snow. Then Aaron turned toward Miriam, and there she was, a leper" (Num. 12:9–10). The leprosy that struck Miriam was not the disease we know by that name, Hansen's disease. Rather, Miriam was afflicted with a disorder that caused her skin to turn scaly and death-like in color.

What God did to correct Miriam may seem harsh to us. After all, she was merely voicing her opinion. But God, and God alone, knew Miriam's heart, and it was her heart that he was seeking to change. God knew that Miriam was resentful of Moses' authority. Miriam, gifted though she was, had not been God's choice of leader, and therefore to speak out against Moses was to speak out against God. It was this spirit of pride and rebellion that God wanted to correct.

Have you ever struggled with resentment like Miriam did here? Perhaps you have been bypassed for a well-deserved promotion and were forced to watch as someone else got the credit for your hard work. Or you may have experienced the humiliation and hurt of being pushed aside or forgotten when you were no longer needed. It doesn't seem to make sense, does it? And it isn't fair. However, fairness of this sort is not something we can expect in this life, nor does the Bible promise it. Instead, we are told to act with godliness in the midst of unfair treatment. That is how Jesus Christ lived out his earthly existence. He is the one who said, "But I tell you not to resist an evil person. But whoever slaps you on your right cheek, turn the other to him also. If anyone wants to sue you and take away your tunic, let him have your cloak also. And whoever compels you to go one mile, go with him two. Give to him who asks you, and from him who wants to borrow from you do not turn away" (Matt. 5:39–42).

That doesn't seem fair. In fact, it is not fair if we evaluate such things from our human perspective. Yet all through Scripture we find examples of things we would call unfair. We witness God arranging circumstances and raising up authorities that, from our limited way of thinking, appear illogical. King David falls into that category. God raised him up, a poor shepherd boy, to be king of all Israel. In the New Testament there is Peter, a lowly fisherman whom God appointed a powerful apostle. God takes a different view about fairness than we do. We may never understand many of the things in our lives that seem unfair, and in those cases, we must rely on our faith that God's ways are higher, broader, and more eternally oriented than ours.

That was the core of Miriam's struggle. She refused to see beyond the scope of her immediate situation, and it made her miserable. Wasn't she equally as qualified as Moses? Had she not proven her courage, her leadership skills, and her heart for God? As the older sister, shouldn't she have been the first choice? All of those thoughts likely brewed within her for some time before breaking out into open criticism.

Unfair Is Everywhere

The same sort of criticism happens in churches today, especially along gender lines. Many women are unable to accept that the pattern set forth in the New Testament indicates that within the confines of the church, men alone are to preach God's Word from the pulpit or hold the role of elder. Some women struggle with that because they know they are equally qualified in terms of education, experience, or intellect—in some cases more so—than the men who hold those positions. An important point to bear in mind if you are questioning this is that the biblical hierarchy has nothing to do with whether or not men are more qualified than women. Those were not the criteria God used in setting up the church system. He appointed men to be over women in some church functions because he knows that most things function better when they operate within a predetermined structure. And within the church, it is Christ, man, woman, in that order, because God set it up that way.

The church is not the only place where Christian women may face this struggle. We hear of unqualified, questionable, or downright undeserving people placed in positions of power in every sphere of society, from corrupt government officials to child abusers in day care or police who brutalize. We confront more mundane yet equally frustrating situations every day, much as Miriam did. It happens when the slacker in the next cubicle gets a bigger raise or when a committee we had hoped to chair gets assigned to the newcomer. In all these cases, we are not given to know why God chooses some when others, including ourselves, appear equally or better qualified.

At heart we all want to be recognized and commended for our personal accomplishments and sacrifices. We have worked hard to achieve them, often pouring ourselves out for the benefit of a cause or an individual. When we are slighted or overlooked, our feelings are hurt and our pride is wounded. Those feelings can suck us down if we fail to look beyond ourselves.

A close friend of mine, although only in her early thirties, has already achieved the distinction of being one of the leading fertility specialists in the world. She is asked to share her research all over the United States and Europe. On numerous occasions during these travels, people sitting beside her on a plane will ask her what she does for a living. Leslie always replies the same way. "I am in the medical profession," she says. Inevitably they look at this young, attractive woman, and exclaim, "Oh, how nice. You're a nurse." Leslie has learned to quell the uprising of indignation and instead smiles in return as she gives a gracious answer. She has learned that God values her work, and that is all that matters in the long run.

Many of you probably experience similar frustration, at home, at work, and in your church, especially if you are a high achiever. The women I know who have experienced the greatest success in their careers seem to have the most difficulty dealing with such frustration.

Of course, there are certain situations where giving away our cloak and walking the extra mile are not the best course of action. We need to speak out against unfairness wherever corruption is rampant. If we truly suspect a civil servant of evil behavior, when someone is raised to a position of authority based on a platform of well-documented lies, when the helpless are getting hurt, then bringing it to light is not only appropriate, it is the right thing to do for the good of all.

However, in matters of opinion, where we feel personally slighted or when our rights have not been acknowledged, the godliest course of action is acceptance rather than anarchy. That is where Miriam failed, and to some degree, why God disciplined her publicly. God did not punish Miriam in such a drastic way in order to further her humiliation. Rather, it was a reminder to Miriam, and to all the people she had disquieted, that God's authority was not to be questioned.

Stolen Superiority

It is clear that the core of Miriam's sin was her resentment of Moses' authority, but that still leaves us wondering why she brought his new wife into her argument. What did the Ethiopian have to do with it? The Ethiopians were descendants of Ham and had been cursed by God back in the days of Noah. Accordingly Miriam's criticism of the new Ethiopian wife may have exposed a deep-seated racial prejudice. We get a clue about that from the manner in which God chose to discipline her, causing her skin to change color through a cursed illness that rendered her a social outcast. We know that Miriam was a woman who loved God, yet prejudice and godliness do not fit together. If that was indeed the case, how was bigotry able to fester in the heart of a woman of Miriam's spiritual maturity?

Think for a moment about the root of racial prejudice. From where does it spring? In some cases it is the sin of self-righteous superiority, but in many other cases it is ignorance. However, the root of most prejudice is fear. We hear stories and stereotypes, and we become afraid. So an instinctive reaction to fear is to crush out what might hurt us in some way, and that is often what is happening when people speak out against a different race, socioeconomic group, or gender. Have you ever wrestled with this issue? If you have not, it is likely you know someone who has.

Whatever the underlying issue that triggers such sin, God does not brush aside bigotry. Miriam's sudden affliction of leprosy indicates that. The disease was so hated that those afflicted were required to remain outside the camp during their illness, warning away others by crying out "Unclean! Unclean!" Miriam was exiled from the camp for seven days before God restored her from what must have been a humiliating experience. God hates any sort of slander that includes racial jokes or stereotyping. All races are welcomed into his kingdom, and by means of Miriam's seven-day ordeal, he made that clear to the entire camp. God, the seer of hearts, is the only one who knows what lay beneath Miriam's criticism of her new sister-in-law; but whether it was fear or merely her determination to keep her place in the camp, it hindered Miriam's ministry and her enjoyment of other people.

Senseless Battles

In spite of Miriam's struggle with these sins, she was not only a godly woman but an accomplished one as well. Today there are more women like Miriam than ever before in history, women with tremendous skills and leadership ability that have been cultivated through education or learned on the job. If you are a woman like that, how do you handle yourself when you feel you have been unfairly bypassed for a good opportunity, one you feel you have earned? Many of us act as Miriam did. We attempt to bring down those we feel are less deserving or those who, however inadvertently, have undercut our sense of worth. We may be blatant about it as Miriam was, or we may be more subtle. We often begin by picking up the phone or walking into the lunchroom, saying, "Oh, do forgive me, but I just have to vent!" Or, "I feel it is crucial that I pass along a few things about Mary."

Where does that get us? Does venting calm our angry hearts? Is Mary brought low because of your gossip? Most often, people see through what we are attempting to do, and they pity us, even as they nod their heads in sympathy. So how do we handle the unfairness of it all in a godly way? We are to take our disappointment, hurt feelings, and sense of unfairness to God. We are always invited to vent our hearts to him.

If God has closed the door on getting you to the top, it is because getting you there was not his objective in the first place. He has great plans and uses for the gifts and talents he has given you. He wants to maximize them. Sometimes when the ladder to success doesn't reach the ceiling, we feel that our usefulness is finished. Not so! It is merely that God's plan for your success differs from the one you envisioned for yourself. Have you been bypassed recently? Are you feeling used or undervalued? If so, you will never find contentment complaining about the unfairness of it all or in trying to get yourself there on your own. Instead, ask God to open new and different channels where you can use your gifts. In the light of eternity, how you used your gifts will count, not how successful you were by worldly standards.

Miriam would have suffered a great deal less if she had turned her heart along those lines. Rather than competing for top place, she could have found contentment by continuing as a spiritual leader for the women in the camp, by leading them on in praise and thanksgiving, and by embracing in love her new sister-in-law. Miriam failed to see that the camp did not need her to be God's spokesman; it had Moses for that. But it did need her in the unique ways she had been gifted and called to serve.

One final sobering reality that we all need to be reminded of from time to time is that, from a spiritual standpoint, we have no rights. Everything we possess is a gift, and when we view it from that perspective, we can enjoy our privileges, forget the slights, and make the most of every opportunity.

9

Rahab

Beauty for Ashes

Hiding the Hurt

"Why don't you ever come to the prayer meeting?" Beth asked Nicole. "Oh, I don't know," Nicole replied. "I guess I just prefer to stay home on Friday nights. I'm too tired at the end of the work week to socialize." A reasonable answer, but in Nicole's case, it was a lie. If truth be told, Nicole was hungry for the company of other Christians.

The excuses began one Sunday not too long ago, when Beth, an active member of the congregation, had intercepted Nicole as she headed for the door after morning worship. She introduced herself. "I've seen you here for several weeks now," she had said. "But you don't seem to know anyone. I'd be happy to help you get plugged in."

Nicole was grateful for Beth, for her kindness and the genuine interest she showed. But getting involved, meeting more people, was a terrifying prospect for her. Every time Beth asked, Nicole would smile and offer a plausible excuse, all the while thinking, "I could never do that!" And she would make her way home from church, lonely, frustrated, and worried that Beth would give up on her.

"If she really knew me, she wouldn't want anything to do with me anyway," Nicole thought. "I can't possibly tell her why I'm afraid to meet other believers. If they ever found out about my life, I probably wouldn't even be welcome in this church!" So Nicole would retreat back into the world where she felt safe, comfortable, and accepted, where rejection was much less of a risk.

Nicole had been introduced to Jesus Christ a few months back during a break at work. While drinking coffee, she had picked up a small New Testament that someone had left on the table in the lobby. With fifteen more minutes to kill, she had flipped through it, opening to the Gospel of John. At the end of her break, a strange hope had burned within her, and the heaviness in her spirit to which she grown accustomed lifted a little. "Can this be true?" she wondered. "Did this one man, this Jesus Christ, really pay for all I've done?" As Nicole went back on duty that day, she somehow knew it would be her last time. If what she'd read was true, how she could work in this place for even one more day?

Nicole awoke the next morning pondering what to do with her discovery. As she thought about it, the church on the corner came to mind, the one she walked by every day on the way to work. Emboldened by the new promise of hope, Nicole had left her apartment and headed for the church. It turned out to be a life-changing day. The pastor there was so kind, even when she told him her guilty secret. He had spent several hours speaking to her about Jesus Christ and how her sins were forgiven because of him. Then he had prayed with her. When Nicole left the church that day she called the supervisor at work and gave immediate notice. She would not be back. The pastor had helped her to understand that a whole new life was beginning. In fact, it had begun that day, and because her occupation was sinful, she was free to walk away and never look back. God would provide everything she needed to live her new life.

Now, several months later, it had all worked out as the pastor had said. She never went back to work, not even to collect her final paycheck. God had provided a new job and a new home, and she had begun to experience the joys of life in Christ. But something was still missing. Nicole longed for companions who fit into her new world. She no longer had any desire for the company of her old crowd. But although Nicole had attended the church every Sunday since, she still knew no one except for the kindly pastor, and now Beth.

Why wouldn't Nicole reach out to take what her heart yearned for? She believed what the pastor said. All her sins—past, present, and future—were forgiven. Her standing before Christ did not trouble her; it was people who scared her. If she let anyone know her, if what lurked below the surface was exposed, she'd die! She could picture what they would say: "You've only been working at the hospital for two months? What did you do before that?" Or, worse yet, "You look awfully familiar. Haven't I seen you coming out of the women's clinic down on 12th Street?" She couldn't say, "Oh, yes. I used to work there as an abortionist's assistant." Could she ever tell them? She knew she couldn't. Ever!

Please Pass the Eraser

Nicole's situation is not unusual. There are many women who live in fear of The Past. Regardless of what it entailed, women who harbor shameful memories have great anxiety about the day when an ugly part of personal history will come screeching out of the closet into the present. All kinds of women can empathize with Nicole's plight, especially women whose lives were formerly characterized by immorality. Oh, they believe that the penalty for their sins has been paid in full by the blood of Jesus Christ. They know they have been cleansed from all impurity and stand in full acceptance before God. But people are not like God. They are not as merciful, or as forgiving, or as kind. Human beings, even redeemed human beings, are prone to insecurities, criticisms, and imperfections that do not exhibit the grace of God. These women fear that their pasts will keep them from the necessary love and acceptance of God's people.

We find such fear in the woman who habitually chooses to date men she generally does not respect. Women with a Past often feel more comfortable with such men because they feel that their chances of acceptance are greater. Women who will not allow anyone to see below their surface because they are harboring unpalatable secrets are quite good at directing the topic of every conversation away from themselves. Lest there be a moment where someone might make a personal inquiry, they have become adept at steering the focus elsewhere. Fear of the past may be masked in any number of ways. What these women lack is an understanding of redemption.

If you are such a woman, you may be thinking, "That is all well and good, but what about the horrible things I did after I was saved? What about those periods of backsliding when I fell away from the Lord and lived sinfully?" God's redemptive work includes those times, too. If you have backslidden, you need not fear returning to God and his people. You do not forfeit his grace because you sin. You miss out on many blessings while you are wandering, but you may step back into them the moment you repent.

If you are struggling with these issues, the story of Rahab should take care of your fears. She was an Amorite woman living in the city of Jericho when she came into fellowship with the people of God. Among all the pagan peoples living in Jericho at that time, the Amorites were among the most wicked. Not only was Rahab a despised Amorite; she was a prostitute. We meet her just as Israel is ready to ambush the city and destroy its inhabitants. The Israelites were lingering on the outskirts of Jericho, waiting for the prime moment to move and conquer the city. Joshua was leading the Israelite tribe at that time, and as part of his pre-attack strategy, he sent two spies into the city to observe the strength of the enemy. These two spies were clever men. They went to Rahab's house to hide—what better place to waylay suspicion than a whorehouse? No one would question the presence of two strangers there. But word got around that two of the feared Israelites were hiding within the city gates, so Rahab the prostitute hid the two spies on her rooftop, and when the authorities came to question her, she protected the Israelites. She merely told the king that two strangers had stopped by her home but had then left the city.

Why would an Amorite prostitute cover up for the spies? She risked her life and the lives of her family members to do so. If her deception had been uncovered, she would have met with a horrible and certain death. We find out her reason after the authorities, being satisfied with her story, departed her house. Rahab went up on the roof and spoke with the men, saying,

> "I know that the LORD has given you the land, that the terror of you has fallen on us, and that all the inhabitants of the land are fainthearted because of you. For we have heard how the LORD dried up the waters of the Red Sea for you when you came out of Egypt, and what you did to the two kings of the Amorites who were on the other side of the Jordan, Sihon and Og, whom you utterly destroyed. And as soon as we heard these things, our hearts melted; neither did there remain any more courage in anyone because of you, for the LORD your God, He is God in heaven above and on earth beneath. Now, therefore, I beg you, swear to me by the LORD, since I have shown you kindness, that you also will show kindness to my father's house, and give me a true token, and spare my father, my mother, my brothers, my sisters, and all that they have, and deliver our lives from death." (Josh. 2:9–13)

The motivation behind the bargain Rahab made was not only to save her life and the lives of her family members. It was instigated largely by her faith in the true God. Look at her words to the spies: "I know that the LORD has given you the land. . . . For the LORD your God, He is God in heaven above and on earth beneath." How did she know that? She knew because her occupation would have afforded Rahab many opportunities to hear about the God of the Israelites. Men from near and far passing through her home each week would have brought news of the world outside the walls of Jericho. Rahab had listened, and her heart had believed. When the spies came, Rahab acted on faith, choosing to side with the people of God rather than those of her city.

No Second-Class Christians

The story of Rahab's conversion shows us that our pasts are no hindrance to God's redemptive work in our lives. God reached out to save Rahab where she was and brought her into his covenant family. Some interpreters have argued that Rahab was no longer likely practicing prostitution when the spies arrived, yet Scripture does not back that. In fact, if Rahab had not been a prostitute, how is it that two men could have used her home as a refuge without arousing suspicion? Where else but at the house of a prostitute would the king have believed the story of two strange men coming and leaving again so quickly?

God actually used her sinful lifestyle as his instrument to save Rahab. He sent the two spies not only to procure Jericho for his people and to destroy the wicked Amorites but also to save Rahab. Not only did he save her soul and save her life; he also brought her into the family of believers. The bargain she had made with the spies went according to plan. She gathered her family at her house and hung a scarlet cord in her window, so when the Israelites came and attacked, she and her family were spared while everyone else in Jericho was destroyed.

Nor was she made a second-class believer because of her previous immorality, but Rahab received a high place in the chosen nation. She married an Israelite named Salmon, and we read in Matthew's gospel that "Salmon begot Boaz by Rahab, Boaz begot Obed by Ruth, Obed begot Jesse, and Jesse begot David the king" (Matt. 1:5–6). If you read through the remainder of Matthew's genealogy, you find that Rahab was an ancestor of Jesus Christ.

If you are a woman with an embarrassing personal history, read through Rahab's story in Joshua 2. You'll find surety that your past is no obstacle to a bright future with the people of God. If God can bring a prostitute into the family tree of Jesus Christ, he will do great things with your life, too.

Goodness and Mercy Shall Follow Me . . .

Perhaps your past is still an all too real part of your present. If you are clinging to a sinful pattern of living inconsistently with life in Christ, if you have one foot with God and his people and the other entrenched in the world because it feels safe, do not let fear of people keep you stuck there. The story of Rahab teaches us how to implement those changes we so desperately need to make but do not make because we are afraid.

Notice how the real changes in Rahab's lifestyle came about when she began living in and among other believers. Prior to that time, she had believed in God, even to the point of risking death for her faith, but she was still living as a prostitute. We read no more about that after Israel entered into Jericho and made Rahab a part of their nation. But she took risks to lay hold of God's blessings. Right where she was, as a prostitute, she poured out her faith to the spies, and asked them to accept her. God had arranged circumstances and hearts so that indeed that would happen, but she first had to expose her real self.

If Rahab had held back in shame and fear, insisting that she had no place with the family of God, she would have perished with the rest of the Amorites. If afterward she had refused to get involved or had continued as a prostitute because "that's all she knew," she would not have become an ancestor of Jesus. In spite of her past, she stepped up, got involved, and became an integral part of the believing community.

We also learn from Rahab that we are free to forget the past and get on with life. Rahab became known as a woman of great faith. If she had given into the temptation to drown in the shame of the past, she might have stayed at least mentally or emotionally stuck there.

Instead, she got on with living a godly life. You can do the same! Put on your new identity as a Christian, and others will begin to identify you by your Christian gifts and graces.

The apostle Paul encourages us by writing, "Brethren, I do not count myself to have apprehended; but one thing I do, forgetting those things which are behind and reaching forward to those things which are ahead, I press toward the goal for the prize of the upward call of God in Christ Jesus" (Phil. 3:13–14).

Paul also instructs us, "But you have not so learned Christ, if indeed you have heard Him and have been taught by Him, as the truth is in Jesus: that you put off, concerning your former conduct, the old man which grows corrupt according to the deceitful lusts, and be renewed in the spirit of your mind, and that you put on the new man which was created according to God, in true righteousness and holiness" (Eph. 4:20–24).

Analyze the verbs Paul uses. We are to *forget* what is past, *reach* forward, *press* toward the goal, *put off* the old, *put on* the new. These are all active verbs, actions we are to practice day by day. Yet even though we are to play an active role in shaping our Christian identity, God does not leave us to do it by ourselves. Paul also wrote, "Therefore, if anyone is in Christ, he is a new creation; old things have passed away; behold, all things have become new" (2 Cor. 5:17). The fact that your old self has passed away is a reality, regardless of how you feel about it. That is why you can be confident that God will enable you to step out and live as the new woman you are.

Finally, Rahab had to swallow her pride in order to get on with the abundant life. The Israelites would have heard the story of Rahab and the part she played in aiding the Jews; and since her prostitution was a key part in the story, all the people, young and old, would have known. Not only was it told all over Canaan, but also her shameful career was written in as part of Scripture in the Old and New Testaments. The book of Hebrews records, "By faith the harlot Rahab did not perish with those who did not believe, when she had received the spies with peace" (Heb. 11:31). But even though everyone knew her past, look at what she is remembered for. It is her faith, not her harlotry. She embraced the believing community and it embraced her in return, and her formerly shameful identity was replaced with one of honor.

No Place for Pride

Swallowing pride about your past means that you can say, "So what if people know!" This doesn't entail a defensive attitude but rather one that reflects confidence that God can glorify himself by means of your past, no matter how ugly it may have been. Romans 5:20 tells us that "where sin abounded, grace abounded much more." That is exciting, because it means that God often uses the dregs of our lives to most bless us and glorify himself. Oh, there will always be those who aren't spiritually mature enough to accept someone with a less than pristine past. But that is their sin, and it cannot ultimately hurt you.

Remember Nicole? She is missing out on so much because of a combination of fear, pride, and shame. What about you? Are you enjoying the fullness of life that God has to offer, or are you hiding in the prison of your past? God does not have good plans for you merely in spite of your past. Rather, he has good plans that actually spring from it.

There are so many women I know of whose lives were previously filled with hellishness of their own making, yet today they are some of the most effective servants for God. When God brings us into the family of Jesus Christ he redeems everything about us. When we become aware of how sinful our former patterns have been, we are able to realize how much we have been forgiven. This in turn gives us empathy and compassion for others' sins. There is no need to hide. Here is Christ's atoning work on the cross for you:

For as the heavens are high above the earth,
So great is His mercy toward those who fear Him;

> As far as the east is from the west,
> So far has He removed our transgressions from us.
> (Ps. 103:11–12)

When God saves us, he takes up everything about us, including our past, and he works it into his good plans for the present and future. Christ's death and resurrection are that powerful! Ask God to make something beautiful out of your past, and he will do it.

10

Delilah

By Hook or by Crook

Beauty and the Beast

Glitzy women's magazines are littered across checkout counters, airports, and waiting rooms. They bombard us every day. We cannot help but read the captions boldly printed on the slick covers, usually accompanied by glossy photos of airbrushed models and current celebrities. The headlines are meant to entice us, and we find ourselves sneaking a glance no matter how much we may scorn them. These popular women's magazines have a similar theme. Can you name it? With titles such as *Self*, *Shape*, *Glamour*, and *Allure*, it is not hard to miss. In a nutshell, these magazines reflect the highest value of today's mainstream women: "Use all you have to get what you want."

Here are some recent headlines: "Outwit Your Mate in Every Argument." "Top Tricks to Make Him Your Slave," "Getting What You Want in Bed," "Make Your Friends Jealous of Your Body." What message do they convey? These magazines are instructing women in the art of manipulation management. It is a message that appears not only on newsstands; we find it in every sphere of life, from college campuses on up to the corporate arena and even in the church.

Has this cultural mandate found its insidious way into your heart? To find out, consider what you do when you want something that you do not currently possess. How do you go about procuring the object of your desire? The most readily available weapon in a woman's artillery is physical charm. Regardless of what we look like, we women have the innate ability to use our femininity to get what we want. A flip of the hair, an arched eyebrow, or a pouted lip can become a sub-conscious reflex over time, and depending on the vulnerability of our victim, such tactics are often effective.

An interesting phenomenon that I have observed, one that has surely existed since Eve, is the way in which hair becomes a prop in certain situations. Long or short, hair is tossed, wrapped around fin-gers, and dangled coyly over the eye in a reflexive attempt to disarm.

Used on other occasions is an air of fragile vulnerability. It works wonders. Since most men welcome an opportunity to assume the role of protector, they will jump to attention when presented with a show of female weakness.

An opposite approach to manipulating others includes all forms of verbal harassment. We are exceptionally good at tailoring tone and pitch to influence people, especially men. All too often it appears as whining or nagging. Grating voices are employed to beat others into submission, because people who are subjected to such tones eventu-ally get to a point where they will do or say anything for silence. Uni-versally, I am sure you would agree, women are more prone to whin-ing or nagging than men. It is an unfortunate trait, the ugly underbelly of femininity. Verbal harassment may also be delivered in a coy remark delivered in a suggestive and promising tone. The implication of reward conveyed in such a tone is often irresistible and much more subtle than haranguing someone into submission through nagging.

Any of these tricks may kick into gear when there is something we want or something we are afraid we may not get. That is because what underlies such behavior is a desperate insistence on having our own way. However, many of us have misused our femininity for so long that we are no longer aware that we do it. That is because the temptation to behave in this way begins as soon as we are old enough to discover its power. I know many two-year-old girls who are already experts! Finally, after years of practice, it becomes a reflex. Can you see yourself here? If you want to find out, objectively observe what you do the next time you ask your supervisor for a raise, when you want to blow the family budget on a new couch for the living room, or when you request after-hours room service from the hotel concierge.

There is no question that, as Christian women, each one of us strives for integrity in our interactions with others. That is why recognizing the art of manipulation in ourselves is often difficult. I am often unaware that I have misused my femininity until after the fact, but I am becoming more aware of those times, such as when I handle my supervisor differently from the way I treat my co-workers. Do you act differently around certain people? If so, where and when do you see your tendency emerging to manipulate? Once you become aware of those situations that kick it into gear, you can seek to identify what it is that you are after.

Whether it is hair, face, figure, or tone of voice, we manipulate because we want something. Furthermore, it is usually something we are not sure that God wants us to have, or worse, something that we know he is against. In those cases, we stop relying on him. In essence we are saying, "God may not want me to have this. But I want it. So I will attempt to get it and worry about God afterward." Most of us do not consciously think such thoughts at the moment, but when manipulative behaviors emerge, those thoughts are undoubtedly there.

A Labor of Lust

For those who do not know God, managing by manipulation is present, in varying degrees, in all their interaction with others. That is because they have no relationship with him and therefore have no idea that he is the great provider. Delilah, from the book of Judges, is a case in point. She was a master manipulator from the Valley of Sorek, a woman loved by the great warrior and Israelite judge, Samson. Judges 16 recounts her manipulative tactics, and it is there that we also discover what motivated her actions.

We read, "And the lords of the Philistines came up to her and said to her, 'Entice him, and find out where his great strength lies, and by what means we may overpower him, that we may bind him to afflict him; and every one of us will give you eleven hundred pieces of silver'" (Judg. 16:5).

Samson was known throughout the land for his great physical strength. No one had been able to defeat him in battle, although he had used his great gift to destroy many Israelite enemies. For that reason, the Philistines were eager to see him crushed, and they were provided with a new strategy when Delilah came on the scene.

Delilah readily agreed to go along with the scheme for the possibility of acquiring all that money. Samson's love mattered little to Delilah. Nor was she insulted that the Philistine lords thought to approach her in this way, assuming that she could be bought. Delilah was a hard-hearted, greedy woman who had no qualms about using what she had to get what she wanted.

If this book were about the men of Scripture, we would focus on Samson here, how his self-centered lusts prevented him from seeing through Delilah's tactics. Guarding ourselves against being manipulated by evildoers is also important. However, since our objective is to learn from the women in the Bible, we will keep our focus on the character of Delilah.

After agreeing to the Philistines' terms, Delilah took advantage of Samson's love with every feminine asset she possessed. She began simply. She said to him, "Please tell me where your great strength lies, and with what you may be bound to afflict you" (Judg. 16:6). Can you picture the scene? Opening her eyes wide, smiling, twirling a piece of hair, perhaps stroking his face, she made the request of her lover. Samson was so captivated by Delilah's charms that her direct exposure of the evil plot failed to alarm him. She didn't even bother to hide it. Then Samson, confident in his strength and delighted by this pretty woman, decided to tease her by fabricating the source of his strength. So confident was Delilah in her power over Samson that she believed his tale. She ran and told the Philistine lords that if Samson were bound with fresh bowstrings, his strength would leave him and he could be subdued. They moved in to attack, but Samson had tricked them all, and Delilah was frustrated. So she stepped up her tactics.

"Look," she said, "you have mocked me and told me lies. Now, please tell me what you may be bound with" (Judg. 16:10). Delilah adopted an injured tone in an attempt to make Samson feel guilty. So he teased her again with the same results. The scene was repeated once more with no success, and finally, exasperated, Delilah said, " 'How can you say, "I love you," when your heart is not with me? You have mocked me these three times, and have not told me where your great strength lies.' And it came to pass, when she pestered him daily with her words and pressed him, so that his soul was vexed to death, that he told her all his heart" (Judg. 16:15–17).

As we can see, when persuasion and charm failed, Delilah abused Samson verbally to get what she was after. The power of whining and nagging lies in its repetitiveness. It beats down the recipient. Solomon wrote about this effect: "A continual dripping on a very rainy day and a contentious woman are alike; whoever restrains her restrains the wind, and grasps oil with his right hand" (Prov. 27:15–16). Solomon knew firsthand of this unfortunate female trait; he had several hundred wives. In Samson's case, such contention, or nagging, "vexed his soul to death." Her whining voice pestered him so severely that he preferred capture and torture at the hands of the Philistines to Delilah's tongue.

Delilah eventually got what she wanted. Samson revealed that the source of his great strength was in his hair. There was nothing magical about his hair but rather in the vows he had taken years before concerning it. Since birth Samson had been a Nazarite, someone set apart solely to serve God. Nazarites were forbidden to shave or cut their hair as a symbol of their special status. So when Samson revealed the secret of his strength and the Philistines bound him and shaved his head, his strength left him. Samson ultimately discovered that the real source of his strength was not his hair but rather the power behind his vow, namely, God. When Samson gave up the last remnant of his vow, God left him.

We cannot, therefore, put all the blame on Delilah. If Samson had been faithful to God, none of her wiles would have been effective. Nevertheless she used her feminine assets and her words as weapons to increase her wealth, and it worked. As we read how the two of them interacted, we wonder how they could have been so blind to what the other was doing, because, as you have likely discovered from your own experience, it is generally quite easy to see these things in other people's circumstances. However, when the situation involves our own emotions we are often equally as blind.

What Lies Beneath

What things tempt you to pull out womanly weapons? In Delilah's case, it was materialism and greed. For women today power and position pose another temptation. In this day and age where women fight for equal rights in the workplace, feminine armory may be put into use when such rights are not readily forthcoming. When legitimate means fail, some women will resort to whatever they can in order to succeed. If obtaining a raise, a promotion, or a coveted project fails to happen as a result of hard work, many women will shorten their skirts and raise their heel height to get it. As Christians we may scorn such actions, but how many of us have freshened our lipstick or joked flirtatiously with a male in a superior position? Subtle actions like that are prompted by the same motivation as more extreme measures.

Perhaps the most common motivator for us is personal attention. When that is what we crave, we are tempted to use our femininity to obtain admiration, sexual attention, and affection. When we are lonely, when our husbands spend more time at the office than at home with us, when the department manager daily bypasses us but stops frequently to talk to the attractive secretary in the next cubicle, we might feel threatened. Those feelings of insecurity, more often than not, kick us into gear. But at heart, any and all misuse of our unique feminine gifts is sin because it is an attempt to put ourselves in God's place.

A right use of feminine assets should not be confused with the misuse of them. Femininity with all its characteristics is not sinful. Far from it! Charm is not by itself a bad thing. In fact, God created us with it already built in, and it is one of the things he uses to unite male and female. A reading of Song of Solomon assures us of that. Yet in our fallen state, we carry it to sinful degrees that God never intended.

Better Than Beauty

All of that leaves us asking, Is there a godly way to go after the things we desire? Indeed there is! It begins with setting our hearts on desiring the things God wants for us. Then when our wills are attuned with his, we will be able to rely confidently on him to take care of us. He has promised to provide us with everything we need. Those who trust that are free to enjoy the unique qualities of womanhood. If God has undertaken to provide for us in every area of life, we do not have to provide for ourselves through dubious means.

That does not mean we can never ask for or work toward something we want. Rather, it is the method of approach we are talking about. If you feel you deserve a raise at work, gather together the reasons why you deserve one, go to your supervisor, and present your case on the facts. If God wants you to get that raise, he will bless your efforts to that end. If you are getting the mere dregs of your husband's time, rather than nagging, sit down with him and discuss your concerns and feelings. In the process, be sure to ask him how he is feeling these days. Perhaps there is an underlying cause for his absence. If so, a well-modulated conversation will reveal it much more readily than any degree of nagging.

Delilah gained nothing for all her skillful manipulations. Oh, she may have been a rich woman, but she was one with a black reputation. Worst of all she was spiritually dead, lost in her sins, relying

solely on herself for every creature comfort. Women like Delilah come
up empty sooner or later. They become hardened, and once that has
happened feminine wiles lose all effectiveness.

Have you ever noticed that many women who are obsessed with
their personal appearance eventually wind up looking overdone and
hardened? What about women who flaunt their sexuality? There is
often a lack of gentleness and respect in how others address them.
And women who nag. Do we honestly think that whining can make
us win? We may berate someone into submission, as Delilah did to
Samson, but those who have to listen will eventually run from us.

The prophet Jeremiah warned about placing inordinate reliance
on feminine wiles when he likened Judah to a harlot:

> "And when you are plundered,
> What will you do?
> Though you clothe yourself with crimson,
> Though you adorn yourself with ornaments of gold,
> Though you enlarge your eyes with paint,
> In vain you will make yourself fair;
> Your lovers will despise you;
> They will seek your life." (Jer. 4:30)

Ultimately there are only two paths on which to direct our feminine selves. We can choose Delilah's path, eventually destroying ourselves and others through a misuse of our personal gifts. Or we can
apply them in the ways God intended and reap great enjoyment from
them. Do you know how to enjoy your unique feminine qualities?
The answer is not complicated as long as it is guided by one thing—
God's glory. If you make that your measure—the standard that moti-
vates all that you say and do—you will know in each situation whether
you are blessing or cursing with your charms.

God wants us to revel in being women, and his word teaches that
as far back as Genesis: "And the LORD God said, 'It is not good that

man should be alone; I will make him a helper comparable to him' "
(Gen. 2:18).

Gifted to Give

God designed us not only as man's helper but also as a *comparable*
helper. Women were created to complement men; in other words,
what men lack, our femininity supplies, and what we lack, their mas-
culinity provides. God therefore equipped women with unique means
to provide a godly influence.

The Bible has a great deal more to say about feminine charm. There
is the example of Esther, a perfect biblical contrast to Delilah. She
used her beauty and every feminine asset she had for the good of others. Reading her story in the book of Esther would be a good way to
follow up this chapter and find personal application. The New Testament also teaches, "Do not let your adornment be merely outward—
arranging the hair, wearing gold, or putting on fine apparel—rather
let it be the hidden person of the heart, with the incorruptible beauty
of a gentle and quiet spirit, which is very precious in the sight of God"
(1 Peter 3:3–4).

I am sure that you, like all of us, desire to be loved, respected, and
appreciated. The world says manipulate others and you will be
admired, envied, and powerful. The Bible says, don't fall for that
because "charm is deceitful and beauty is passing, but a woman who
fears the LORD, she shall be praised" (Prov. 31:30).

11

Naomi and Ruth

Surprised by Sacrifice

Twists and Turns

After two lonely years in New York City, Susan's life was looking up. The change from small-town living to the impersonal, transient nature of New York had been overwhelming that first year. Susan had spent many a homesick night alone in her tiny apartment on the Upper East Side. But the opportunity to work at a world-famous auction house had been too good to pass up. Two years later, on this bustling New York Saturday, Susan walked through the park with a joyous heart, glad that she had persevered. She loved her job and was beginning to carve out a reputation in the industry.

Not only that, her phone was ringing more frequently these days. Trying to make friends in a large urban church had taken effort. It wasn't like the church back home where members pounced on visitors to enfold them into the congregation. Here in New York a newcomer had to take initiative, and it took time. On this bright morning Susan looked forward to the hours ahead. Errands along now familiar streets, lunch with two girlfriends later, and tonight a dinner party with more new friends from church. Far from the loneliness of those first months, life was exciting now. Susan was here to stay.

But in the same way that bad times eventually turn around for good, times of bliss do not roll endlessly on either. Just when everything in life is going beautifully, something comes in to unsettle the hard-won balance of our lives. Susan's life changed on that Saturday, not many weeks after all the pieces had fallen into place. It happened about five o'clock that afternoon when she picked up the phone to place an overdue call upstate to her mother.

Susan's widowed mother lived alone in a large, old house just below the Adirondack Mountains where Susan had grown up. She had visited several times since moving to the city, and each visit confirmed the choice she'd made to leave there. She loved her mother, but small-town life held little stimulation for a young, artistic, and urban-minded woman. Susan glanced at her watch while she waited for her mother to answer. She'd have to hurry. The dinner party was all the way across town. Much to Susan's surprise, her mother's neighbor, an old family friend, answered the phone. She sat in shocked silence as the neighbor exclaimed relief that Susan had called. He had been trying to locate Susan's phone number and was in the process of searching her mother's desk when the phone rang. Could Susan come home right away? Her mother had had a stroke and was hospitalized, partially paralyzed and unable to talk.

Susan's thoughts raced and clashed. "Oh, no! My mother is alone. God, please help her! The party! Now I won't be able to go, and I so wanted the opportunity to get to know everyone better. And what about work on Monday? How can I go away right now?" In the midst of mental turbulence, Susan called to express her regrets to the party host, packed a bag, and commuted to the airport in time to catch a flight early that evening. Little did she realize then that the upcoming weeks would bring her face to face with the hardest decision of her life.

As Susan's mother began a slow, painful recovery, it became apparent that much of the stroke damage was permanent. Members of her mother's church and residents from the neighborhood had reached out to help, knowing that the aging woman was alone. Susan's visits to her mother in subsequent weeks were painful. Her newfound social life was on hold, and she felt selfish for even thinking about it when her mother was so ill. Not only that, the visits were hard because she felt silent rebuke from her mother's helpers that she wasn't there every day.

As the end of her mother's hospital stay drew near, those helpers spoke up in open criticism. Where would this lonely and disabled woman go now? She was not well enough to return home alone, and she had no other relatives, nor could she afford at-home health care. Her needs exceeded the capabilities of her church friends and neighbors. Susan wanted to help her mother in every way she could, yet how could she do that and continue to build her new life in New York City?

The Best Laid Plans . . .

What would you do in Susan's place? Maybe you have had to face the dilemma that occurs when a relative or close friend requires more of us than we have to give, sometimes to the point of disrupting the structure of our carefully balanced lives. Susan visited her pastor for advice, and he directed her to the book of Ruth in the Old Testament. It contains the story of two women named Ruth and Naomi whose lives God had interwoven. Just like Susan, Ruth and Naomi each had a difficult choice to make, one of two paths to pursue. For both of those women, one of those paths held out the promise of peace and personal fulfillment, while the other path denied such fulfillment because it led to the singular well being of someone else. All of us try to tailor our lives so that those things are not mutually exclusive. We strive to work things out for the happiness of ourselves and others simultaneously.

Sacrificing what we want to do so that someone else may benefit is the definition of duty. Duty has negative connotations in this age of self-centeredness. But sooner or later in varying degrees duty beckons to each one of us. Through the course of prayer and wise counsel, Susan discovered where duty lay in her particular situation. It entailed giving up her life in New York City, at least for the time being, to return home to care for her mother.

What enabled Susan to understand the harder path as the right path, in her case, was an assessment of all the facts. Guilt would have been the wrong reason for her decision, as would the indignation of her mother's friends. Rather, she was able to list concrete reasons why returning home was the best way to serve God. It was while Susan meditated on the book of Ruth that direction became clear.

In the book of Ruth, we find two young widows, Orpah and Ruth, who lived with their widowed mother-in-law, Naomi, in the land of Moab. As we have been learning, unattached women did not fare well in the ancient Near East. They needed the protection of father or husband to ensure survival. Yet these three women derived great comfort from one another. The husbands of all three had died within a short time, and the intimacy born through shared grief bonded the three closely together. Yet, Naomi, as head of this all-female household, feared for the future safety of her daughters-in-law if they were to remain with her. She knew they would fare better if they started over with new husbands.

Not only that, Naomi wanted to go home to Israel. Some years back her husband had taken her away from Israel in order to escape famine, but he had not lived to bring her safely back home. While in Moab, their two sons had married women from that region, women from a people who did not believe in the true God of Israel. After the deaths of her sons, Naomi was left with little godly companionship, in spite of how bonded the three women had become. She longed for the company of others who shared her faith.

So Naomi decided to return to Israel alone, determining that Ruth and Orpah would fare better without her. She said to them, " 'Go, return each to her mother's house. The LORD deal kindly with you, as you have dealt with the dead and with me. The LORD grant that you may find rest, each in the house of her husband.' So she kissed them, and they lifted up their voices and wept. And they said to her,

'Surely we will return with you to your people.' But Naomi said, 'Turn back, my daughters; why will you go with me? Are there still sons in my womb, that they may be your husbands?' " (Ruth 1:8–11). In spite of her downcast heart, she was able to think of the welfare of Orpah and Ruth. She could easily have played on their sympathy, coaxing them to remain with her in her loneliness, but she did not.

Drive and Determination

The idea of parting was painful for Naomi, but she knew that her decision was a sound one. Naomi would be with her people once again, and the girls would have a better chance of remarrying if they remained in Moab. That left Orpah and Ruth with their own choices. Would they remain with their mother-in-law, or would they go on to build new lives? Orpah chose the latter, but not Ruth. She refused to leave her mother-in-law, in spite of Naomi's insistence.

The choices made by Ruth and Orpah revealed the true state of their hearts. Both young women loved Naomi; however, Orpah's heart had remained with the Moabites, their customs, and their gods, whereas Ruth's heart had come to believe in the true God of Israel. Additionally, she was loath to leave her desolate mother-in-law. Initially Orpah's choice appeared to be the wisest. She was heading back to sure safety and a greater possibility of starting over. Yet Orpah's practicality was superficial, based solely on material provision. Ruth's decision was not impractical; however, in her case it was a practicality that sprang from spiritual considerations rather than worldly ones. Ruth could have done what Orpah did by placing her material welfare first and abandoning her suffering mother-in-law, but she believed she could help Naomi by remaining with her.

No more is heard of Orpah; the story follows Naomi and Ruth from that point on. The two went back to Bethlehem in Israel and were welcomed by Naomi's kinsman. It is at this point that we discover what Ruth and Orpah must have been well aware of—that Naomi was in a deep depression. She said to those who greeted her,

"Do not call me Naomi; call me Mara, for the Almighty has dealt very bitterly with me. I went out full, and the Lord has brought me home again empty. Why do you call me Naomi, since the LORD has testified against me, and the Almighty has afflicted me?" (Ruth 1:20–21).

Naomi's name means "pleasant." At this low point in her life, such a name seemed merely a mockery of better days. She asked to be called Mara, a name meaning "bitter," because it was a more accurate reflection of her heart then. Naomi was downcast not only at the death of her husband and sons but additionally, through all that had resulted from those deaths, she had developed a negative view of God. That negative view was the cause of her depression.

Yet in spite of Naomi's downcast heart, she focused on the future welfare of her daughter-in-law as she reestablished herself in Israel. Meanwhile, Ruth went to work in the fields to provide them both with food. As the two began a new daily routine, a man named Boaz, a relative of Naomi, came into the picture. If that name sounds familiar, it is because we read about Boaz earlier. He was the son of Rahab. It was in his field that Ruth set to work and where Boaz first became aware of this young widow, and from the story it is evident that Ruth was immediately drawn to this kindly man.

Naomi, witnessing the budding relationship, developed a plan to bring Ruth and Boaz together. At the same time she was well aware of the Jewish law, the law of the kinsman-redeemer. In Israel, if a man died leaving a wife, the closest unmarried male relative was required to marry the widow in order to produce children in the name of the dead relative. The law was also established to afford protection to the woman. Naomi knew that Boaz, being a relative, fit the requirements to assume the role of kinsman-redeemer for Ruth. She kept silent on the matter, however. If a union between Ruth and Boaz could come about naturally, why impose the law? Additionally, there was another male more closely related to Naomi, and if she were to call the law into play, that relative might interfere by stepping up and assuming his legal responsibility.

Rather than spending her energy on making her life better, on relieving her suffering, Naomi devoted herself to bringing about a match between Ruth and Boaz. She told Ruth,

> "My daughter, shall I not seek security for you, that it may be well with you? Now Boaz, whose young women you were with [in the field], is he not our relative? In fact, he is winnowing barley tonight at the threshing floor. Therefore wash yourself and anoint yourself, put on your best garment and go down to the threshing floor; but do not make yourself known to the man until he has finished eating and drinking. Then it shall be, when he lies down, that you shall notice the place where he lies; and you shall go in, uncover his feet, and lie down; and he will tell you what you should do." [Ruth answered,] "All that you say to me I will do." (Ruth 3:1–5)

Ruth followed Naomi's leading, not only because she wanted a new husband but also largely out of deference to her mother-in-law. Submitting to one's elders was an indication of respect and great affection. It may appear that Naomi's scheme flies in the face of all the Bible says about feminine decorum, about waiting for God, against plotting and scheming to bring about our goals. Motivation is what makes the difference here. Each woman was acting primarily out of love for the other.

Motive Makes the Difference

Such motivation is pleasing to God, and he blesses the lives of those who are willing to sacrifice for someone else. That is evidenced in this story in Boaz's initial attraction to Ruth. Early on she asked him why he was attracted to her, and he replied, "It has been fully reported to me, all that you have done for your mother-in-law since the death of your husband, and how you have left your father and your mother and the land of your birth, and have come to people whom you did not know before. The LORD repay your work, and a full reward be given you by the LORD God of Israel, under whose wings you have come for refuge" (Ruth 2:11–12).

Not only was Boaz drawn to Ruth by her devotion to Naomi; he was also aware that she had committed herself to God and his ways at great personal cost. And God did reward Ruth. In a short time, Boaz and Ruth were joined in marriage. Ruth's future was secure, she had a man she loved, and she lived among the people of God.

Naomi, who had chosen to focus on Ruth's welfare rather than her own, was honored for her sacrifice also. She was far past the age where a man would marry her for childbearing; she faced a perilous old age. But after Ruth bore her first son to Boaz, we read, "Then the women said to Naomi, 'Blessed be the LORD, who has not left you this day without a close relative; and may his name be famous in Israel! And may he be to you a restorer of life and a nourisher of your old age; for your daughter-in-law, who loves you, who is better to you than seven sons, has borne him' " (Ruth 4:14–15).

Nothing to Lose

Two women whose lives were intertwined were used by God, each for the other. If either had panicked in their difficult circumstances, if either had adopted the attitude, "I have to take care of myself," they would not have seen how God blesses those who forsake their needs for another. The blessings for Ruth and Naomi were not finished. In fact, they would continue for decades to come. Ruth's first son, Obed, became the grandfather of King David, therefore making Ruth an ancestor of Jesus Christ.

Reading the story of Ruth and Naomi encouraged Susan to give up her flourishing life in New York to take care of her mother. What lies in store for her remains to be seen, but God will surely provide for her. Susan has come to believe what she cannot yet see: that as she concentrates on taking care of another, she is moving aside to allow God to take care of her. That is true of us, too. When we are wrapped up in securing our own happiness, we only get in God's way.

I live in a small apartment, so when I entertain I prefer to do the cleanup afterward by myself. That is because when others get in the kitchen it is too crowded. Inevitably someone knocks into someone else and a dish gets broken. I am freer to move about and get everything back in order when there are fewer hands involved in the process. Just so with God's work in our lives. We often feel that we need to help him out, that he is not able to handle matters. In reality, our attempts to help often delay or harm what he is working out for us.

Maybe you are facing a situation somewhat like Susan's. Perhaps in your case, it is a friend rather than a family member who needs your sacrificial care. Have you become aware of a pressing need in the life of another? You might have a friend going through a time of sorrow or grief, one who is lonely and needs extra attention. Someone you know may be shut up at home in sickness, or perhaps it is someone facing dire financial problems. Are you in a position to help? Maybe you are, maybe you are not. But the disruption of your personal space, hard-earned luxuries, and carefully constructed schedule should not be the determining factor. On the other hand, guilt and legalism are also wrong reasons to jump in. Just because a need presents itself is not an indicator that duty calls you.

Susan made her determination based on sound counsel and biblical principles. In her case, her mother had no other options. That is a vital factor to consider. Someone may want you to come to the rescue at great detriment to your own welfare when that person has multiple means of help. Another thing to consider is the work you are currently doing for God. If you have a sense that your life today is positioned where you are best called to serve him and sacrificing for another may call you to forsake that, it may be an indicator that supplying the need of that other person is not falling upon you. That is where talking to a pastor or another mature Christian can bring clarity.

There are other factors that can help you know that God is most likely not calling you to a course of duty outside the scope of your present life. If the sacrifice would remove you from all fellowship with other believers, it is wise to be doubtful about proceeding. For Ruth and Naomi, the path of personal sacrifice furthered their interaction with the people of God.

If the course you are considering is unbiblical, you can be sure it is not God's will. If your boyfriend breaks both legs and loses all mobility for a time, you are definitely not called to move into his apartment to care for him. Even if it appears that there is no one else to help him, you can be confident that you are not God's provision for him in this circumstance.

The call to self-sacrifice, perhaps more often than in any other situation, happens when our parents age and lose their self-sufficiency. Sooner or later many of us face the choice of what to do when they become ill or feeble. In those cases, a biblical understanding of the value of all sorts of human relationships helps us make good decisions. For example, Scripture commands us, "Honor your father and mother, that your days may be long upon the land which the LORD your God is giving you" (Exod. 20:12). It also says, "Wives, submit to your own husbands, as to the Lord. For the husband is head of the wife, as also Christ is head of the church; and He is the Savior of the body. Therefore, just as the church is subject to Christ, so let the wives be to their own husbands in everything" (Eph. 5:22–24). Will bringing an aging parent to live in your home bring friction to your marriage? Although God places a high premium on the honor we owe our parents, the marriage relationship holds a higher priority from a biblical standpoint. That must be worked through first in order to determine your duty in that type of situation.

On a lesser scale, we have countless opportunities to sacrifice for others daily. When the telephone rings in the middle of a project, it is sacrificial to stop what we are doing to engage in the interests of the caller. When our children are in need of attention, it is a sacrifice to forego our adult enjoyments to meet them on their level. When co-workers interrupt the flow of our work, it is sacrificial to respond graciously, holding irritation at bay.

In the little issues as well as the big, God takes note and rewards those who wisely seek, find, and live out a life of sacrifice for others. If you are facing a life-changing call to duty, or even a minor inconvenience sometime this week, consider another ahead of yourself. You have nothing to lose; God will see to that.

12

Hannah

Forget Me Not

One True Friend

Do you have an ideal friend? Such a friend is someone who keeps your deepest secrets, always rejoices when good things come your way, and shows compassion when you are grieved. An ideal friend never berates you when you make a mess of things or says, "I told you so." Such a friend is available any time of the day or night to listen to you when you have an urgent need to talk and never grows tired of hearing about the same old things over and over again.

Too good to be true? On a human level, yes. For who among us knows someone who always upholds us or never gets impatient or distracted with other matters? And who among us extends that degree of kindness to another, one hundred percent of the time? Only God is an ideal friend. He will never betray us, he delights to bless us, and he grieves when we mourn. God delights when we share every aspect of our lives with him, and he is infinitely patient with our faults. In fact, God longs to be your ideal friend, but the depth to which you experience his friendship depends largely on you.

Just as in all rewarding relationships, enjoying God comes from being in his presence and getting to know him. Alongside his Word, the more time that you spend with God in prayer, the more your enjoyment of the relationship grows. You will find yourself experiencing its benefits in every facet of life. You will know immediately where to turn for help when trouble comes. In times of difficulty you will find desperately needed comfort ready at hand, because you are already practicing the presence of God. It is a fact that those who meditate infrequently on Scripture and pray only sporadically miss out on experiencing many aspects of this most special of all friendships.

No Holding Back

Hannah was a woman who knew how to pray. She was married to a godly man named Elkanah, and in their home observance of the law and all matters pertaining to worship were observed. But life was far from perfect for Hannah. She shared her husband with another wife named Peninnah. Hannah had a problem we've encountered with other women in Scripture: she was unable to bear Elkanah any children. The fact that this other wife was fruitful in that way only added to Hannah's misery. Like Rachel before her, she was the more beloved of her husband in spite of her barrenness, yet Elkanah's love failed to console her.

Surely Hannah had prayed about this matter for a long time, yet no answer was forthcoming. Finally she felt she could endure her suffering no longer. In despair she wept and refused to eat. Nevertheless, she traveled with her husband up to Shiloh to offer sacrifices to God and worship him. While in Shiloh, Elkanah sought to comfort his wife. He said to her, "Hannah, why do you weep? Why do you not eat? And why is your heart grieved? Am I not better to you than ten sons?" (1 Sam. 1:8). After he had spoken with her, Hannah shared a meal with her husband. Perhaps his words brought her a small measure of momentary comfort; or maybe she felt badly that her sorrow caused him to suffer also.

In either case, after they had eaten, Hannah went to the temple to pray. There she gave full rein to her sorrow. While "she was in bitterness of soul, and prayed to the LORD and wept in anguish," she cried out, "O LORD of hosts, if You will indeed look on the affliction of Your maidservant and remember me, and not forget Your maidservant, but will give Your maidservant a male child, then I will give him to the LORD all the days of his life, and no razor shall come upon his head" (1 Sam. 1:10–11).

There are several things to learn about prayer from Hannah's words. First, this is the sort of prayer offered by someone who knows God intimately. Those who do not know him well tend to pray with stiff formality, regardless of the pain they may be experiencing. The same principle is true in human relationships. The way we communicate sorrow to a close friend is very different from how we express ourselves to a mere acquaintance. Hannah obviously felt comfortable enough in God's presence to pour out all her emotions along with her deepest desires.

Another thing to note is the respectful attitude toward God that Hannah displayed in the midst of great heartache. God had the ability to change her situation at any time, but he had not done so. Yet rather than complain, rather than blame God for leaving her barren, Hannah prayed with humility.

Hannah's prayer also exhibits boldness. She asked that God would "look upon her," that he would "remember her," both requests for personal favor and blessing. Additionally she was specific in her request. Not only did she pray for a child; she asked God to give her a boy.

Finally, Hannah made a vow to God. She offered the hoped-for son to the service of God. Hannah promised that this son would be a Nazarite all his days. Do you remember who else was a Nazarite? Samson, Delilah's lover, was one too. Nazarites were men especially set apart for God. Certain restrictions were imposed upon these men in order to illustrate their status to the community. They were forbidden to drink alcohol or go near anything from which they might become defiled. They were also to avoid cutting their hair. That is

what Hannah was referring to in her prayer when she promised that
no razor would ever come upon her child's head.

The Real Purpose of Prayer

One thing that we are not to infer from Hannah's prayer is the
making of bargains with God. Offering God something in exchange
for what we want from him will not in any way increase our chances
of getting that for which we hope. God did not work that way with
Hannah nor does he work that way with us. Rather, he has said, "For
I desire mercy and not sacrifice, and the knowledge of God more than
burnt offerings" (Hos. 6:6). And, "Has the LORD as great delight in
burnt offerings and sacrifices, as in obeying the voice of the LORD?
Behold, to obey is better than sacrifice, and to heed than the fat of
rams" (1 Sam. 15:22).

The reason we do not need to make bargains with God is that Jesus
Christ paid every debt we will ever incur when he suffered and died
on the cross for us. We receive everything we have because Jesus
already made a vow and offered the sacrifice of himself. There is therefore nothing greater that you could offer on your own behalf. You are
free to ask from God what you wish, and you can expect to receive
back because your obligations have all been met, if you have claimed
Christ's sacrifice for sin as your own.

While Hannah was praying, the priest of the temple, Eli, witnessed
her tears and saw her lips moving but he could not hear what she said.
He mistakenly concluded that she was drunk, so he came over to
rebuke her. Aghast, Hannah said to Eli, "No, my lord, I am a woman
of sorrowful spirit. I have drunk neither wine nor intoxicating drink,
but have poured out my soul before the LORD. Do not consider your
maidservant a wicked woman, for out of the abundance of my complaint and grief I have spoken until now" (1 Sam. 1:15–16).

Upon hearing her explanation, Eli spoke words of great encouragement to Hannah: " 'Go in peace, and the God of Israel grant your
petition which you have asked of Him.' And she said, 'Let your maid-

servant find favor in your sight.' So the woman went her way and ate, and her face was no longer sad" (1 Sam. 1:17–18).

We learn two important points from this exchange between Eli and Hannah. First, spiritual strength and encouragement flourish through our communion with other believers. Although time alone with God is crucial to every believer's walk of faith, God designed us to be in company with one another. We see Hannah practicing both while in the temple. She shared the depths of her heart with God alone, quietly. Afterward she shared her spiritual condition with Eli. Notice that it was after both events that her face was no longer sad. Fellowship with another believer served to reinforce her confidence in God.

Another important observation is the fact that Hannah "went her way and ate." She got up from her knees and resumed her life. This was an indication of trust in God's care and ability to answer her prayer. If after we have turned an important matter over to God, we continue to indulge in our misery, worries, or anxieties about the issue, it is a sign that we have not truly left it in his hands. Yet the only way we are able to do that is by determining to let God decide how best to answer. Hannah's response shows that she was willing to accept whatever answer God saw fit to bring her.

Is there a key area in your life over which you have serious dealings with the Lord? Something you yearn for painfully but for which no answer has yet been forthcoming? If so, how are you handling yourself while you wait for God? Have you left the matter with him and moved on with your daily life, or are you still anxious about the outcome? Maybe you are saying, "I cannot help but be anxious. I have no guarantee that God will give me what I want. The Bible doesn't specifically promise me the thing I hope for." That may be true. There are many things for which we hope that are not specifically promised in Scripture. But one thing you can be sure of is that God will answer in the best possible way, whether or not it is the specific thing for which you asked.

God's best is not like medicine—good for us but rather unpalatable. He promises that we will never be disappointed with his order-

ing of our affairs. Dr. James Montgomery Boice wrote, "If we determine to walk in God's way, refusing to be conformed to the world and
being transformed instead by the renewing of our minds, we will not
have to fear that at the end of our lives we will look back and be dissatisfied or bitter, judging our lives to have been an utter waste. On
the contrary, we will look back and conclude that our lives were well
lived and be pleased with them."[1]

Once knowing this, if you are still anxious, it may well be that you
are not truly willing that the outcome of the matter be God's arrange-
ment. It may be a sign that underneath you are still insisting on your
own way. If that is the case, pray about that, too. Ask God to soften
your resistance. If you do, he will work to change your unwillingness
so that you will be able to accept with joy and peace the answer he
has to give.

In Hannah's case, God's answer for her was that for which she had
asked. We read, "So it came to pass in the process of time that Hannah conceived and bore a son, and called his name Samuel, saying,
'Because I have asked for him from the LORD' " (1 Sam. 1:20). Note
that God did not answer her immediately but rather "in the process
of time." That should encourage us to wait for God and not give up
because we cannot see anything happening as a result of our prayers.
God will not forget.

When All's Said and Done

Once we have received an answer to our prayers, there is something we all too often forget, and that is to praise and thank God for
what he has done. When someone you love brings you a gift, carefully selected and beautifully wrapped, what do you do? Do you rip
off paper and ribbons and immediately set about using the gift without a word of thanks to the giver? Of course not! You express your
gratitude to the loved one for his or her thoughtfulness and follow up
with a note in the mail. Perhaps you have known how it feels to give

someone a gift that is never acknowledged. If so, you know all too well how that hurts!

Hannah responded with a prayer of praise and gratitude:

> "My heart rejoices in the LORD;
> My horn is exalted in the LORD.
> I smile at my enemies,
> Because I rejoice in Your salvation.
> No one is holy like the LORD,
> For there is none besides You,
> Nor is there any rock like our God." (1 Sam. 2:1–2)

Hannah's prayer of thanksgiving continues for ten verses of 1 Samuel 2. It is a good deal longer than her initial outpouring of grief and petition, an interesting thing to note about the ratio of praise to petition. Hannah's praise also shows us how much God had changed her as she waited for his provision. The focus of this later prayer of praise is centered on God rather than on herself. She praised him for his power and his sovereign control over everything that comes to pass. She exclaimed,

> "He will guard the feet of His saints,
> But the wicked shall be silent in darkness.
> For by strength no man shall prevail." (1 Sam. 2:9)

She attributed her newfound happiness not to the son she has borne but rather to the fact that she belongs to God. Through the valley of waiting, God had taught her to understand that he alone is the underlying source of all joy, much more so than the things he gives us.

Divine Delay

All of that shows us that God has a purpose in making us wait for the answers to many of our prayers. It is through waiting that the fruit

of patience is born in our hearts. It is no exaggeration to say that waiting is often an occasion of suffering. When we long for something
and have waited sometimes years for God to step in, there is pain
involved. But that sort of pain is what God often uses to conform us
to the image of Christ—his ultimate goal for all his children. And
the more Christ-like we become, the happier we will be.

Think back to Hannah's spiritual and emotional doldrums when
we first met her. We read that Hannah was characterized by anguish,
grief, and sorrow to the point of utter misery. At the point of her
prayer of petition in the temple and the comforting words spoken
by Eli the priest, Hannah began to change. That is because God was
already at work to fulfill her petition, although in a way she could
not see or understand at the time. It was as if God were saying, *Hannah, I know how badly you want a child. I am going to give you what you
desire, but first you need to learn that having a baby is not really what will
make you happy. Only I am that source. So I am going to work true happiness into you as you await my provision, even though you do not understand what I am accomplishing. But when you have your child, you will
not mistakenly think it is he who is responsible for your joy. You will know
that it is I.*

At what place in Hannah's story do you find yourself? Perhaps you
are where she was in the beginning of the story—in a state of miserable despair. If so, you can go to God and tell him everything on your
heart. We are invited to bring every yearning, each unfulfilled desire,
to his listening ear, compassionate heart, and capable hands. Are you
frustrated? Discouraged? Angry? Is there an unmet yearning weighing
you down? If so do what Hannah did. Bow before him and pour out
your heart. After you have done so, share your burden with another
believer whose spiritual walk you value. Ask him or her to pray with
you. Then get up and go your way, leaving the matter in God's hands.

Perhaps you have already done that, and as Hannah did, you are
waiting for God to answer. Do not lose heart! Even if you cannot see
how God is working out your particular situation, you can rest assured
that he is operating behind the scenes to "do exceedingly abundantly

above all that we ask or think, according to the power that works in us" (Eph. 3:20).

I have a close friend who learned this truth about God in her life through her desire to find a life's companion. For years she felt just as Hannah did before she relinquished her request into God's keeping. A large portion of her time was consumed with her desire so that her daily life was frequently blanketed by anguish. Some days she would pray for a husband, while on others she asked God to remove her intense yearning if marriage were not his will for her life. Nothing changed. The desire remained, but no companion appeared. She waited, and waited, and waited.

Over time she has come to understand God's great love for her in this long process. By withholding her heart's desire, God has allowed her a good deal of suffering, yet it is through that suffering that God has most worked to sanctify her in the ways of holiness. She used to pray, "God, can't you pick a different means to teach me your ways? Why must it be through this thing that I want so badly?" But she knows now that if it had been something else, something that mattered less, the resulting benefits would also have been far less.

She is still waiting for God's complete answer to that long-ago petition, yet now, today, there is no anguish. Through waiting, and, yes, suffering, God has brought her to a place where she knows true happiness. Whether or not he gives her a companion in this lifetime has become of secondary importance to my friend. That is because she has found where true happiness lies, something she would not have learned if God had immediately given her what she thought would make her happy. She knows now that the best life has to offer rests with God who lives *in* her, and that realization has become even better and more important than someone who can exist *beside* her.

God wants to bless us with the strength and obedience that come through waiting. The prophet Isaiah wrote,

Even the youths shall faint and be weary,
And the young men shall utterly fall,

> But those who wait on the LORD
> Shall renew their strength;
> They shall mount up with wings like eagles,
> They shall run and not be weary,
> They shall walk and not faint. (Isa. 40:30–31)

And,

> Therefore the LORD will wait, that He may be gracious to you;
> And therefore He will be exalted, that He may have mercy on you.
> For the LORD is a God of justice;
> Blessed are all those who wait for Him. (Isa. 30:18)

The picture may be very different for you. At this moment you might be living in the bliss of desire fulfilled. If so have you taken time to praise God, not only for the supply he provided but for all he accomplished within you in the process? You might want to set aside some time to offer up Hannah's prayer in 1 Samuel 2 as your prayer.

In all things, at all times, and in all his ways, God is the friend of those who come to him through Jesus Christ, and you will find that when you open yourself fully to him, prayer is the means of experiencing that to the fullest. It stands as God's personal invitation to you and to me.

> Trust in Him at all times, you people;
> Pour out your heart before Him;
> God is a refuge for us. (Ps. 62:8)

13

Michal

A Royally Dysfunctional Family

Days of Our Wives

The family of King David was, undoubtedly, the most dysfunctional family in biblical history. Given the adultery, incest, betrayal, and murder that characterized the clan, God's grace is evidenced in how powerful Israel became under David's authority. The time of David's rule followed by that of his son, Solomon, was the pinnacle of Israel's history. During his kingship, the Jewish nation became a superpower, and it held sway over the Near East until the death of Solomon.

David, however, had a difficult rise to power, largely because his rival, King Saul, sought to destroy him at every turn. David made Saul look bad, and Saul hated him for it. But David triumphed over every obstacle, each challenge, and all of Saul's death threats. It was perhaps for this reason that Saul's daughter Michal fell in love with David.

She had many opportunities to observe this young, handsome man, one who was able to outwit her father, the king, at every turn. Not only was David strong and attractive; he also had a mark of power. God had blessed him in all to which he set his hand. David was the sort of man who appeals to young women yearning to throw off a restrictive parental yoke. Saul cursed him constantly at home and abroad, spewing forth his jealous hatred, and Michal would surely have overheard much in her father's angry ravings.

Michal set her heart on David, so much so that her father got word of it. But in spite of his intense hatred toward David, Saul seemed pleased by Michal's interest and, surprisingly enough, he agreed to bring about a marriage. But Saul's motives weren't pure. He was less interested in the affections of his daughter's heart than he was in destroying David. Saul was obsessed. In fact, in his scheming mind he had already considered such a marriage as a way to regain control, if not with Michal, then through another of his daughters. Through such a marriage, Saul could make another attempt at destroying his rival.

So Saul told David that he would agree to a marriage, but before David could have Michal, he would have to perform an act of loyalty for the king. David would have to slaughter 100 Philistines, potent enemies of the Israelites. Saul was sure that David could not succeed, that he would surely die in the attempt, and he would be rid of his young nemesis. But against all odds David succeeded in slaying the Philistines, thus furthering Saul's hatred but procuring the king's daughter as the first of his many wives. We read, "Then Saul gave him Michal his daughter as a wife. Thus Saul saw and knew that the LORD was with David, and that Michal, Saul's daughter, loved him; and Saul was still more afraid of David. So Saul became David's enemy continually" (1 Sam. 18:27–29).

Once she was married, however, Michal's romantic notions were rapidly undermined. She found herself in the middle of the bitter conflict between husband and father. One night Michal got word of another of Saul's murderous plots against her husband. She ran and said to David, "If you do not save your life tonight, tomorrow you will be killed" (1 Sam. 19:11). So David, with Michal's help, worked quickly to escape the impending danger—a secret task force sent by Saul to kill David in his sleep. While the enemy poised for attack outside, Michal lowered David out of the window to the ground below where he escaped safely into the darkness.

When Saul discovered the deception and the role that Michal had played in helping David, he was furious, thus rendering Michal in a perilous position. This was not just her father whom she had betrayed; he was also the king of Israel. Helping David escape was treason, an act for which death was an appropriate penalty, king's daughter notwithstanding. To cover her tracks, Michal lied to her father. She told the furious Saul that David had threatened to kill her unless she helped him escape. Under the circumstances it is hard to blame her for that lie. David had fled she knew not where, leaving her to stand up to the king alone.

The marriage was off to a rocky start, and Saul was only a fraction of their ensuing problems. David and Michal were impulsive and self-centered, as the story reveals later on, traits not conducive to marital bliss. And in the meantime, Saul continued to plague the young couple. Over time he went so far as to take Michal away from David and give her to another man, Paltiel.

While David waited for a strategic occasion to get Michal back in his home, he took several additional wives. Although this was in direct violation of Mosaic law, it was regular practice for ancient Near Eastern kings to marry many women, largely for the purpose of forming alliances with neighboring territories. Although doing so may have strengthened David's political position, it harmed him spiritually and brought calamity upon his family, as the breaking of God's laws inevitably does.

As Saul's bitterness and hatred toward David grew, he became increasingly more volatile until, not surprisingly, he eventually lost his kingship and died in disgrace. Afterward, an opportunity arose in which David was able to regain his first wife, and Michal was brought back to him. Love was an unlikely motivation on David's part. The opportunity that had enabled him to reclaim his wife also served to strengthen Israel's place in world politics, likely a primary motivation for David in making the deal. Nowhere are we told that he loved her. As far as David was concerned, we can only infer from the story that Michal was a political pawn in the power struggle over Israel. It sounds cruel and hardhearted to us, but that sort of practice was the accepted custom of the time, especially among those of high official standing. So David was reunited with his first wife, and she lived with him once again alongside all his other wives.

Over time David's power grew, and he became king over all of Israel as God gave him victory to overcome obstacles one by one. As David's power strengthened, so did his devotion to God, something that he expressed in visible ways. From the psalms and other records found in the Old Testament, we know that David was a gifted musician and writer and that he used those talents to lead Israel in public worship. It was this very thing, however, that brought about the destruction of his relationship with Michal.

Marital Hiss

On the day of David's crowning achievement—the arrival of the ark of the covenant in Jerusalem—David led Israel in offering praise to God. The stone tablets containing God's law had been brought safely home to Jerusalem, the city from where David ruled the nation. It was a glorious moment in Israel's history. The people of the city followed David as he danced in thanksgiving, accompanying him with shouts and the sound of trumpets. But Michal did not participate in the worship that day. We read, "Now as the ark of the LORD came into the City of David, Michal, Saul's daughter, looked through a window and saw King David leaping and whirling before the LORD; and she despised him in her heart" (2 Sam. 6:16).

What does it mean that she "despised" David? It means that Michal felt contempt as she witnessed her husband the king acting in a decidedly unkingly manner. Michal felt humiliated and embarrassed by her husband's actions, and she confronted him as soon as he arrived at home. Her voice dripping with sarcasm, she said, "How glorious was the king of Israel today, uncovering himself today in the eyes of the maids of his servants, as one of the base fellows shamelessly uncovers himself!" (2 Sam. 6:20).

Michal was referring to the fact that David had removed his kingly garments in order to dance more freely, leaving himself covered by only a linen cloth called an ephod. Michal was upset for two reasons. First, other women had seen her husband in a state of partial undress. She was already required to share her husband with other wives, and now having other women glance at the scantily clad, handsome king would naturally inflame her already jealous heart. Even more apparent is the fact that David's dancing embarrassed Michal. She felt that David had made a fool of himself, and thus of her, by laying aside even momentarily the outward symbols of his authority.

Michal's confrontation reveals the true state of her heart. Although her jealousy is understandable, her embarrassment stemmed from decidedly ungodly motives. Michal's tone of ridicule indicates that she cared more for appearances and for her social standing than she cared for God's glory. What seems apparent is that Michal's love for David was an immature love, one that developed purely from the aura of power he emanated. Thus, when he put off the visible signs of his authority, the foundation of her love disappeared.

Michal's sarcastic contempt was the death knell of her marriage. We read, "So David said to Michal, 'It was before the LORD, who chose me instead of your father and all his house, to appoint me ruler over the people of the LORD, over Israel. Therefore I will play music before the LORD. And I will be even more undignified than this, and will be humble in my own sight. But as for the maidservants of whom you have spoken, by them I will be held in honor.' Therefore Michal the daughter of Saul had no children to the day of her death" (2 Sam. 6:21–23).

The Bible does not tell us whether barrenness came upon her instantly as a punishment from God or whether David refused to be intimate with her ever again. Regardless, the Bible does portray Michal in the wrong.

Stuck with a Slouch

How many of us, in our own way, commit the same sin and fool-ishness that Michal did! Many of us marry for the wrong reasons, only to realize later that we wish we had waited. Michal found David appealing largely because her obstinate and foolish father feared this attractive young hero. David also appealed to her youthful ideas of romance, but that was hardly the foundation on which to choose a marriage partner. Most women, to some degree, are attracted to pow-erful men. Monica Lewinsky's affair with Bill Clinton typifies that fact. And why is it that corporate executives, when choosing second and third wives, so easily acquire young and attractive women? It is the authority and power such men exude, a potent aphrodisiac to young women seeking stability and instant status.

Another probable reason why Michal married David was to escape a chaotic home life. Her father was volatile, easily prone to murder-ous rages against even his family members. He was spiritually unsta-ble to the degree that, on one occasion, he turned to occult practices (see 1 Sam. 28:3–25). And finally, Saul committed suicide. The home of Michal's youth was hardly an environment where a young woman could flourish.

Many women today also marry to escape a difficult home life or other troublesome circumstances. We know that in the beginning Michal respected David, however superficially, and respect is a key element in choosing one's husband. In fact, it is a biblical mandate. But other factors must be considered, too. Michal had failed before-hand to take into account the inevitable difficulties that would result if she married her father's worst enemy. Family issues, among many others, must carry weight when a woman is deciding whether to marry.

Perhaps you find yourself in Michal's situation. You have come to realize that you married for the wrong reasons or chose poorly. Are you determined to honor God and obey Scripture by remaining in a less than ideal marriage? We confronted a similar challenge when we looked at Hagar's situation in chapter 3. Michal had no choice in the matter; however, today, walking out of an unpleasant marriage is an attractive option for many women. Maybe you are tempted to leave your husband because divorce seems like the only solution to your marital troubles. But if you are a Christian who wants to please God, you do not have that choice. If you are facing that temptation, you can find strength in realizing that God knows everything about your struggle and is there to help you.

Countless women, over time, have lost respect for their husbands. If you are among them, the love and attraction that you once felt has withered away. If that has happened to you, your marriage is hanging on a shaky precipice. But God always blesses obedience, so if you are remaining in a disappointing marriage in order to please God, sooner or later he will bless you in it. The apostle Paul wrote, "And let us not grow weary while doing good, for in due season we shall reap if we do not lose heart" (Gal. 6:9).

Hung Up on Hang-Ups

In Michal's case, however, it was not lack of judgment that destroyed her marriage. Rather, it was her prideful embarrassment at David's public display of worship. Michal was more concerned about maintaining a dignified image than she was in offering uninhibited praise to God. And then, to make matters worse, she mocked David for placing God ahead of his own kingly stature. She sought to humiliate her husband for his worship practices. Perhaps you are thinking, "Well, that's a relief! My marriage may have its problems, but I would never treat my husband like that!" But Michal's sin is more prevalent among us than we might first think, even if it shows up in more subtle ways. We can know we are guilty if our spouse's legitimate, legal, and biblical behavior causes us to feel shame, embarrassment, or humiliation.

A woman I knew some years ago, Elaine, struggled with this sin. She was married to a man who made use of every opportunity to share the gospel. A bus driver, a waitress, unsaved family members, and countless others were all treated to the message of salvation in some form or fashion. Rather than commending him for his boldness, Elaine was embarrassed and treated him much as Michal treated David. She could not accept that his candid proclamation of the gospel was his way of offering love to God. He was frequently rejected for his out-spoken faith, and on those occasions when she was present, she experienced the rejection too. She felt humiliated, yet she convinced herself that her husband's approach to evangelism was wrong.

Perhaps your husband does something to honor God that embarrasses you. Maybe he prays too loudly or too long in restaurants. Perhaps he presses your comfort limits by waving his hands during hymn singing. And to cap off your frustration, those are possibly the traits you found appealing when you first met him! Initially they conveyed to you his deep, spiritual character, but now you find those traits merely irritating. If so, God will help you handle your irritation. However, the chances are good that change will come from within your heart and attitude rather than any outward change in your husband's personal style. God was pleased at David's display because it was for the express purpose of glorifying him. God was not pleased with Michal, because her feelings were all about herself.

A wife may also feel embarrassed by her spouse's behavior in matters other than worship. A friend of mine, Aileen, experienced a good deal of marital strife over the way her husband dressed. Before they were married, Aileen didn't seem to mind his clothing, or at least she never expressed her dislike. But after they were married it became a major point of contention. Aileen finally realized that the problem was her attitude. She admitted, "I hated the way Jed dressed and sought to change that because I figured that after we had gotten married, all his actions became reflections on me!" God helped Aileen to see that such thinking was self-focused. From that point on, she repented, and eventually her irritation with Jed ebbed away.

Not So Minor Matters

I recall hearing an encouraging story on this very issue over the radio some years back. It went something like this: A woman considering marriage to a kind and loving man could not make up her mind to marry him because his personal appearance embarrassed her. His clothes rarely matched; he had no knack for putting himself together. She had prayed and prayed that God would change him. "God, if only he would dress differently, I could be attracted to him! How can I marry a man with whom I am ashamed to be seen?" But God remained silent, and nothing changed. But she cared about this man and did not want to give up.

On the advice of a friend, the woman began praying in a different way. She asked that God would change her attitude about his appearance. She prayed, "God, please help me to accept this good, godly man just the way he is. I do not want something as superficial as clothing to keep my heart from him." It wasn't long after she prayed that her boyfriend came to her and said, "You know, I don't think I like this suit and tie. Would you come shopping with me and help me find something else? I've never been very good at this sort of thing. I hope you'll be willing to help me." That woman learned an important lesson. God was not about to bless her when she was most concerned about her self-image, but he readily stepped in when she was willing to forego her self-concern for the sake of something much more important.

Notice that God did not consider her problem trivial. He cares about the things that distress us, no matter how insignificant they may be. Perhaps in your case, it is not clothing. Maybe you married a man whose grammar makes you cringe or one who has less education than you and your friends. Whatever it may be, the first step toward marital harmony in the matter must be the opposite of Michal's approach toward David. Sarcastic confrontation will change nothing but will only add to your misery and his. Is it a small thing, something that sounds too petty to mention? If so, you can always take it to God in prayer. There is nothing too small for his attention.

If your discontent stems from something more weighty than merely that of attire, your best bet is to pursue open communication with your husband. In fact, doing so is a necessity. Rather than plowing him over with criticism, ask God to pave the way for you with regard to how you address the problem. Pray also for your husband's receptivity. Still, even if it is a matter involving your husband's relationship with God, as was Michal's case, ask God to change your heart first. In fact, that is a good way to begin praying about any issues that cause you embarrassment in your marriage. Take to heart the words of the apostle Paul, "Wives, submit to your own husbands, as is fitting in the Lord" (Col. 3:18). If you are willing to have your heart changed, you may be joyfully surprised at what God will do in your marriage.

14

Abigail

A Woman's Touch

Brute Force

"What an unlikely couple!" Cara couldn't help but overhear the whispered comment. The whispering woman and her escort had assisted Cara in getting her husband, Nate, out to the car and into the back seat where he was now sprawled, passed out from alcohol. Cringing, Cara rolled up the car window so she wouldn't hear more of their conversation. It wasn't as if she hadn't heard it before, but it always hit her with a fresh jab of humiliation. Cara did everything she could to avoid social events with Nate. Over the years his drinking had gotten worse, and even on those occasions when he consumed no alcohol, he was loud, rude, and belligerent. He deliberately made provoking remarks to anyone who displeased him, and trouble would inevitably ensue unless Cara was at his side to smooth things over. He was even hostile and rude to her in front of others.

Finding excuses to keep Nate at home was the easiest way to avoid social situations. Oh, he was just as nasty to Cara at home as he was in public, but at least there she didn't have to feel the shame of other people's pity. Cara had scrambled desperately for a plausible excuse to decline this wedding invitation, but it was the marriage of the daughter of Nate's boss, and naturally Nate had insisted that they attend.

Upon arriving at the reception, Nate had gone straight to the bar. Cara could tell that one of his bad moods was already brewing. Apparently he had felt slighted due to an offhanded remark made by a colleague on the receiving line. As Nate belted down drink after drink, his voice got louder and his tone became jeering. Then, just when Cara thought the situation couldn't get any worse, Nate had made an inappropriate, crude, and rancorous remark about the bride. Silence fell over the cluster of guests standing nearby, and much to Cara's horror she saw that Nate's boss, the bride's father, was in their midst. Gracious host that he was, he had made no comment, but his face reddened in anger, and he turned on his heel and walked away.

Cara wanted to die. Not only had Nate made a fool of himself; he had unquestionably jeopardized his career, their sole source of income. Cara no longer needed a polite, evasive excuse to leave the reception. Others were glad to see them go. She lay hold of Nate's arm, forced a smile onto her face, and whispered, "We're leaving. Right now!" Her frantic tone only angered Nate, who rebuffed her urgent pleading. At that moment an observant couple had quietly approached, asking if she needed help. Holding back tears, Cara accepted. Together they persuaded Nate to leave, and they helped her get him out to the car. After a word of embarrassed gratitude, Cara slipped behind the wheel. It was just before she drove off that she heard the woman mutter the all too familiar comment, "What an unlikely couple!"

Cara and Nate are an unlikely couple. Where Nate is clamorous, Cara is generally tranquil. His often hostile disposition contrasts with her gracious demeanor. Cara's generosity offsets Nate's stinginess. But at the core of their differences is the fact that Cara has been saved by Jesus Christ while Nate is perishing in his sin. People wonder how they ever got together.

Marriages like this are all too common. For that reason, it is likely that you know a godly woman who is married to an unbeliever. Perhaps that woman is you. Such mismatches come about when a believer falls in love with an unbeliever, and rather than face the pain of breaking off the relationship, the believer goes ahead with a marriage in the hope of bringing the unbeliever to faith. Mismatches are also found with couples who married before either one was saved, then sometime after the marriage one spouse became a Christian while the other did not.

If you are a Christian woman existing in such a marriage, you are likely familiar with the loneliness, the frustration, and the monotonous pull of regret. If you acted foolishly by choosing to marry an unbeliever, by now you likely understand all too well the Bible passages that warn us against these unions. You can relate to Paul's words: "Do not be unequally yoked together with unbelievers. For what fellowship has righteousness with lawlessness? And what communion has light with darkness? And what accord has Christ with Belial? Or what part has a believer with an unbeliever?" (2 Cor. 6:14–15). Every time you hear that passage, you despise yourself. You lament, "Why didn't I listen to friends, to family, to the pastor, to God!"

If you became a Christian after your marriage, you may not have that awful sense of regret, but the future paints a bleak and dismal picture in your mind. You probably know from memory the words of the apostle Paul: "a woman who has a husband who does not believe, if he is willing to live with her, let her not divorce him" (1 Cor. 7:13). For many women who read that verse it is like hearing a death sentence.

Abigail and Nabal: A Marriage of Adversity

There is good news, however. If you married an unbeliever, you are not necessarily doomed to a life of misery, nor have you thwarted God's ability to make something unique and valuable out of your situation. We can be confident of that because the Bible does more than merely warn us away from trouble and exhort us to make the best of a bad bargain. It also holds out hope for women who find themselves in such marriages. That hope is there to discover when we read the story of Abigail, a gracious and beautiful woman who was married to a boorish, brutal idol worshiper named Nabal.

Scripture is silent about how Abigail came to be married to such a man. Very likely hers was a marriage arranged by her father, according to the custom of the day. Nabal was wealthy, and that fact would have overridden his less desirable qualities in the eyes of Abigail's father. Regardless of how the marriage came about, the union was not a happy one. Abigail faced an even more grim future than Cara does because, unlike Cara, women then had few means of personal protection from spousal abuse.

The women we have looked at so far were written into the Bible's narratives because they all played a specific role in redemptive history. In this case, Abigail and Nabal are brought into Scripture because their paths cross the path of David, a key figure in God's plan of redemption. At the time of their story, King Saul was still in power. You may recall that those were perilous years for David, years when he was forced to hide in order to protect his life from the jealous king, who was also his father-in-law through his marriage to Michal. Over time, David had acquired a large band of followers, about 600 in number, and together they sought places to hide from Saul and his troops. It was during one of those periods of exile that David encountered first Nabal, then Abigail.

Nabal was a prosperous farmer. In his employ were many shepherds and farmhands who worked out in the fields tending Nabal's livestock, and these employees had dealings with David and his followers as they moved secretly through the wilderness. While conversing with Nabal's farmhands, David learned about this prosperous farmer, so when his group was in need of food, David sent ten of his men to humbly ask Nabal for provision. Nabal was well able to help David, but he refused. Scripture says that Nabal "reviled" David's men, which means that not only did he refuse but also he shrieked at them in outrage.

When David got word of Nabal's refusal, he became angry and vowed revenge on him and his household. David prepared for attack; meanwhile, one of Nabal's wise servants ran to Abigail and told her the story. In urgent tones he said to her, "Look, David sent messengers from the wilderness to greet our master; and he reviled them. But [David's] men were very good to us . . . Now therefore, know and consider what you will do, for harm is determined against our master and against all his household. For he is such a scoundrel that one cannot speak to him" (1 Sam. 25:14–15, 17).

In most cases if a servant were to speak against his master to his mistress, there would be dire consequences later. But the fact that the servant felt free to do so is indicative that the household knew the truth about Nabal and Abigail. Just like Cara in her marriage to Nate, Abigail's gentleness and godly attitude remained constant in the midst of great shame. From the fact that the servant went to Abigail for help, we can infer that she was no weak or light-minded woman but one whose reputation was well established throughout the large household. The servant knew they could count on her to make a plan, take charge, and attempt to stop the pending destruction that Nabal's boorishness had brought upon their home.

And, indeed, Abigail acted quickly. She had the wisdom to know that the angry David and his men would be more apt to listen to reason if their hunger were first appeased. She packed a good supply of rich food and wine, loaded it on donkeys, and set out to meet the angry renegades. She hid her actions from her husband, however, which in this case was a wise course of action. Abigail knew that when a choice must be made between obedience to God or obedience to man, God's way is the only acceptable choice. Additionally, as a woman of true faith, Abigail knew that David was under the special protection of the God of Israel and that any attempts to harm him would be thwarted.

With meekness and likely much fear, she came upon him:

Now when Abigail saw David, she dismounted quickly from the donkey, fell on her face before David, and bowed down to the ground. So she fell at his feet and said: "On me, my lord, on me let this iniquity be! And please let your maidservant speak in your ears, and hear the words of your maidservant. Please, let not my lord regard this scoundrel Nabal. For as his name is, so is he: Nabal is his name, and folly is with him!" (1 Sam 25:23–25)

The name Nabal literally means "fool." Since it is unlikely that any parent would give a child such a name, Nabal had probably acquired it as a sort of nickname by reputation. Abigail, still down on her knees, continued her appeal. She pleaded with David for mercy. She told him that she knew God was his defender, and she believed that God had destined David for great things. Abigail cleverly concluded her humble speech by pointing out that if David slaughtered her household in vengeful anger, he would be ashamed of himself later.

Her words pierced David's heart, for he said, "Blessed is the LORD God of Israel, who sent you this day to meet me! And blessed is your advice and blessed are you, because you have kept me this day from coming to bloodshed and from avenging myself with my own hand" (1 Sam. 25:32–33). So David took her peace offering of food and wine and sent her home to Nabal.

If your marriage is anything like Abigail's, you will be able to empathize with her. A woman whose husband drinks excessively has most likely been trapped in the humiliation of seeking pardon from those her husband has wronged, cleaning up his messes, and taking his blame on herself. The same is true for women whose husbands, in whatever way, are living solely for themselves with total disregard for God or for their family. If you are married to an unbeliever, at some time, to varying degrees, you have likely experienced something of Abigail's life with Nabal. But hope for Abigail was about to dawn, and if you are in a bad marriage, there is hope for you, too.

Abigail returned home to find Nabal drunk and gorging himself on food. She wisely said nothing of her encounter with David, rightly judging that apprising Nabal of the day's happenings while he was inebriated would not result in a constructive conversation. Experience told her that Nabal would most likely fly into a rage upon hearing her tale.

However, the story takes a life-changing turn the next day: "So it was, in the morning, when the wine had gone from Nabal, and his wife had told him these things, that his heart died within him, and he became like a stone. Then it happened, after about ten days, that the LORD struck Nabal, and he died" (1 Sam. 25:37–38).

Most likely, upon hearing that his wife had gone against his wishes, Nabal got so angry that he had something like a severe stroke that left him paralyzed. He died just over a week later, and from the way the story is told, we know that God had judged this wicked man, thus freeing Abigail from his control. And not only was Abigail free; a new life was about to begin for her: "So when David heard that Nabal was dead, he said, 'Blessed be the LORD, who has pleaded the cause of my reproach from the hand of Nabal, and has kept His servant from evil! For the LORD has returned the wickedness of Nabal on his own head.' And David sent and proposed to Abigail, to take her as his wife" (1 Sam. 25:39–40). She gladly went forth to marry David, a man who was not only the future king of Israel but also one whose heart was wholly dedicated to God.

Until Death Us Do Part

Abigail's story ends with the sort of deliverance for which anyone in her situation would hope. I dare say that women who are married to men like Nabal do, at times, subconsciously or even secretly wish that their husbands would just disappear from the face of the earth. Maybe you, in a similar situation, have had those thoughts, though you would never voice them to anyone. Or there may be times when you wish for your own death. If so it is because such marriages, with the fear that accompanies them, also produce a despair and hopelessness from which death seems to offer the only solution.

You can take solace in knowing that just as God came to the aid of Abigail, he will help you too. The help that he provides you may be much less visible or dramatic than that which Abigail received, but it will be tailored to your circumstances. If you find yourself in desperate need of God's help in your marriage, the way to find it is to live like Abigail. It is through day-to-day obedience and in personal godliness lived out before your unbelieving husband that you will find it.

Paul offers direct encouragement to women who are married to unbelievers. He instructs them to remain married to their husbands, and then he adds, "For how do you know, O wife, whether you will save your husband? Or how do you know, O husband, whether you will save your wife?" (1 Cor. 7:16). Paul is saying that by remaining in your marriage, thereby allowing your husband to witness your godly conduct, it may be the instrument God uses to bring your husband to faith.

Camilla, an elderly, Christian woman, has been married to an unbeliever for decades. She and her husband have four grown children, not one of whom is yet a professing Christian. Camilla has dedicated her life to exhibiting the love of Jesus Christ in her home. Her husband's rebuffs and gruff attitude toward her faith have not quenched her determination. Over the years, the family has suffered multiple tragedies, including the untimely death of two grandchildren, one from a sudden and brief illness and another in a car accident.

Despite it all, Camilla and her husband have remained together all these years. And gradually, as one sorrow after another has rocked the family, rather than rebuffing Camilla, her husband has begun to soften toward her. He asked if he could accompany her to church one Sunday recently, and it was all Camilla could do to keep from crying as he held her hand through the service.

Sometimes, as in Camilla's case, we are required to wait years to see any results from our obedience. Occasionally we will not see it, not in this lifetime anyway. But often, if we are willing to live out the sort of patience and perseverance required under such circumstances, we will experience the fruit of our labors. Women who remain with unbelieving husbands are making a sacrifice, not only for their unbelieving spouse but, even more importantly, for God. If you are married to an unbeliever, you have, to a large degree, found your life's calling. And if you follow it, you will know God's hand of help and strength in a way that might have been impossible otherwise.

A bit of hopeful encouragement is found in the book of Ecclesiastes: "What profit has the worker from that in which he labors? I have seen the God-given task with which the sons of men are to be occupied. [God] has made everything beautiful in its time. Also He has put eternity in their hearts, except that no one can find out the work that God does from beginning to end" (Eccl. 3:9–11). Whether or not you can see how your godly conduct is making any difference, God is surely working behind the scenes through your sacrifice.

Some women find themselves married not only to an unbeliever but also to one who is physically abusive, or an alcoholic, or a gambler. Abigail lived every day in that kind of situation. Women today have more options; we can provide for ourselves if the need arises. In situations where your physical welfare, or that of your children, is jeopardized, a separation is a wise option to consider. Or, if remaining legally married would prove physically harmful, as might be the case of a woman married to a gambling addict, a divorce may be the only means you have to protect your family. But even if that last resort is necessary, which it rarely is, in order to continue to exhibit godly conduct, you are not at liberty to remarry someone else.

Hope for the Hurting

Maybe you, a Christian, are at this moment contemplating marriage to a man who does not have a personal relationship with Jesus Christ. I hope you are having second thoughts. If you are hesitating because the wedding is all planned, the invitations have already been mailed, and your family wouldn't understand, getting out now is still your best option. It may be the most painful thing you have ever done, but in the long run it will not be nearly as painful as a lifetime married to someone with whom real intimacy as God intended is impossible. It is never too late to change your mind until you say "I do."

If you are cherishing hopes that you will change your man once you are married, you will be disillusioned later on—ask just about anyone you can find who got married with that same false hope. But today you still have a chance. As long as you are not yet married, no matter how far along the relationship may have progressed, you are free. Once you have made your vows, remaining in that marriage becomes God's will for you; you are joined to that man for life.

The apostle Paul gave the Christians at Corinth some sobering thoughts about uniting with unbelievers in any significant way. He wrote, "Do not be unequally yoked together with unbelievers. For what fellowship has righteousness with lawlessness? And what communion has light with darkness? And what accord has Christ with Belial? Or what part has a believer with an unbeliever?" (2 Cor. 6:14–15). According to Paul, if you marry an unbeliever, you are marrying lawlessness, darkness, and satanic influence.

If Paul's words apply to you, if you are considering marriage to an unbeliever, you can decide to get out, even if you don't think you can do it. God is not standing over you as a stern judge. He is not saying, *Well, you got yourself into this mess, so you'll just have to find your own way out.* Far from that, God will come to your aid now. He will provide you with the courage and all the other help you need in order to be obedient to him.

We know that this is true because Paul backed up his warning to the Corinthians with these words that he adapted from the prophets Jeremiah and Ezekiel:

> "I will dwell in them
> And walk among them.
> I will be their God,
> And they shall be My people."

Therefore
"Come out from among them
And be separate, says the Lord.
Do not touch what is unclean,
And I will receive you."
"I will be a Father to you,
And you shall be My sons and daughters,
Says the LORD Almighty." (2 Cor. 6:16b–18)

If you will take God at his word and believe that whatever he has in store for you is better than marriage to an unbeliever, he will show you that he is worthy of your trust. He wants you to be able to look back at the end of your life and determine that his ways were ways of peace and blessing.

For all of us—those married to an unbeliever, and for those contemplating getting into that situation—remember Abigail. Life with Nabal was a daily hardship, mostly because there was nothing of God guiding his thoughts, his actions, or his heart. His orientation to life was self-focused and based on worldly impulses. A wise pastor once pointed out that we all have one of two spiritual fathers, one being God and the other being Satan. You do not want Satan for a father-in-law. There is no neutral ground. Keep that in mind if you are considering marriage to an unbeliever. If you already find yourself there, remember what God did through Abigail. He used her suffering as a tool to beautify her character and to glorify himself, and at the last, he delivered her into a better place.

If you are bound to your own Nabal, God can and will make you beautiful through your suffering, beautiful to your unbelieving husband and to those all around you. Those who choose to live lives of obedience in the face of great suffering come to know a peace, a joy, and a contentment that usually comes no other way. And, at the last, whether it be in this life or the next, God will set you free.

15

Gomer

A Real Heartbreaker

An Affair to Remember

"Did you hear about the Johnsons?" Amanda asked as she poured Meg's coffee. "They are getting back together! Can you believe it?"

"How can he take her back after all she did to him!" exclaimed Meg.

"It's been three years since she walked out, leaving him alone with those three kids," Amanda added, "and she wasn't exactly discreet with all those men, either."

"I should say not," said Meg. "She flaunted her affairs all over town. I can't believe how hard-hearted she's acted all this time. Even when her children begged her to come home, she turned a deaf ear."

"Not only that," Amanda continued, "about a year ago I heard she got in some sort of legal trouble and racked up a lot of debt."

"Her husband's a saint," Meg went on. "He intervened to get her out of that mess. Did she even thank him? No! Just kept right on living the high life."

"Personally, I think her husband is a fool to even think about taking her back," said Amanda. "She's here now only because her new friends vanished when her money ran out. She's broke with nowhere to go. I think he's crazy to even let her in the door!"

"Well, he loves her. He always has, no matter what she's done," Meg said. "People thought he was a fool to marry her in the first place. But that's true love, I guess."

The words of Amanda and Meg echo conversations that likely took places centuries ago in the northern kingdom of Israel, chatter about Hosea and his wife, Gomer. That is because, at God's instruction, Hosea had married Gomer, a woman who later abandoned their home, shamed Hosea in the community, and scorned his love. It is a tragic story, and as we hear it, our hearts break for Hosea. We wonder why God would lead him into a marriage like that. God did it because Hosea was a prophet, one of God's appointed messengers, sent to warn Israel about coming judgment. Hosea was God's representative, and Hosea's marriage was to serve as a representation of the relationship between God and the Israelites at that time. Hosea's prophecy is like a pageant, a dramatic portrayal, yet a real-life drama nevertheless. Just as Gomer did to Hosea, God's people had been scorning his love through unfaithfulness and abandonment.

Some years into the marriage Gomer deserted Hosea, leaving him with three children to rear by himself. The thrill of new lovers was intoxicating to Gomer, and she gave herself over to men who lived to have fun and lavished upon her luxuries of every kind. Overwhelmed by grief and anger, not knowing what else to do, Hosea attempted to get her back by appealing to her maternal instincts. He first sent his children to rebuke their mother, but to no avail. Gomer was wrapped up in her new life, a pleasure-oriented, materialistic existence. She said, "I will go after my lovers, who give me my bread and my water; my wool and my linen, my oil and my drink" (Hos. 2:5).

Over time, Gomer's reputation grew more and more tarnished in the community. No longer was she thought of as the wife of the prophet Hosea. She was a harlot, a cheap woman who had slept all over town. At first there had been plenty of men for the taking, rich men who found the wild Gomer exciting. They wined and dined her;

she was a conquest well worth the effort. As time wore on, however, her glamour wore off. A loose woman's charms are soon tarnished; Gomer had become hardened and used up. As she moved from one man to another, her lovers changed to men who ranked low on the socioeconomic scale of Israel. They did not shower her with gifts, fine food, and wine of the best vintage. She was reduced to settling for men who could barely put clothes on her back and a meal on the table. And since Gomer made no secret of her shameful life, Hosea witnessed much of her illicit activity. Yet in spite of his great pain and betrayal, he kept his eye on her, watching out for her personal welfare. As he witnessed her decline and saw that she lacked basic necessities like food and drink, he found a secret way to supply her basic resources from his income. Gomer did not know what her husband was doing. She assumed her lover of the day was providing those things, and the lover was likely all too glad to let her think so.

Finally, when Gomer had spiraled down to a state of poverty and despair, her life with Hosea began to look good again. She said, "I will go and return to my first husband, for then it was better for me than now" (Hos. 2:7). But ultimately Gomer did not go back, and things went from bad to worse. Eventually Gomer found herself poverty-stricken and homeless, so she was sold into slavery.

It was at that point that Hosea's love was once again put to the test. He recounted, "Then the LORD said to me, 'Go again, love a woman who is loved by a lover and is committing adultery. . . .' So I bought her for myself for fifteen shekels of silver, and one and one-half homers of barley. And I said to her, 'You shall stay with me many days; you shall not play the harlot, nor shall you have a man—so, too, will I be toward you' " (Hos. 3:1–2).

Hosea was forced to purchase his wife as a slave off the auction block. What a shameful day for that couple. Back then slaves were presented naked to prospective buyers. And though hardened by sin, Gomer's form was, in all likelihood, still quite pleasing. Bidding for this naked and disgraced woman may have been fiercely competitive. But Hosea kept at it until he outbid all the competition. Finally, for fifteen shekels of silver and some barley, he became the legal owner of his wife. As a slave owner, Hosea had procured the right to do whatever he pleased with Gomer, including putting her to death for shaming him with her adultery. But he did not. He forgave Gomer and took her back home.

Would you have been as forgiving of your spouse? Forgiveness like that seems impossible to us, and it is, apart from God's help. We shudder in horror at the mere thought of such betrayal. When we hear about women like Mrs. Johnson and Gomer, we rack our brains trying to understand how they could act that way. Living in this present age, you have surely experienced or witnessed a home breaking apart, a family shattered when one spouse decides to walk out for a new life. The anguish caused by that spouse's selfishness often ripples down for generations.

To most of us, such selfishness seems incomprehensible. But the truth is that we are all capable of sin like that. In fact, we commit spiritual adultery every time we sin because, as Christians, we are married to God, bound to him by the same sort of covenant that accompanies marriage. You may not have walked out on your family, although perhaps you have. Yet no matter what sinful things you have done and still do, they are the same in God's eyes as what Gomer did to Hosea. Understanding that truth is the whole purpose behind Hosea's story. It is the reason why three chapters of Scripture are devoted to his marriage.

Lovers, Liars, and Ultimate Losers

From this story God wants us to understand that when his people sin, they commit adultery against him. He is forced to watch us as we give ourselves to other gods. Our sin evokes his jealousy and his grief. But, like Hosea with Gomer, God never stops loving us. He longs for our return and will go to great lengths to bring us back home.

You may be thinking, "I don't give myself to other gods. I am committed to Jesus Christ!" But when you understand what idolatry is, you will see that you do. When we come across idol worship in the Bible, we read about wooden statues and bronze castings with names like Molech and Astarte, river gods and fertility goddesses. That is what we often think of when we consider the idea of idolatry. But although those ancient idols have passed from the picture, plenty of new ones have taken their place. In our culture alone there are numerous gods. There is the god of Power, and the god of Materialism. Many people bow down to the goddess of Sex. Probably the most potent idol worshiped in our culture is the god of Self. We, as Christian women, are not exempt from the temptation to worship such idols. And even if we do not commit adultery with these gods, we flirt with them from time to time.

Most women who cheat on their husbands do not wake up one day and decide, "I think I'll go out today and find a new man with whom I can have some fun." More typically, adultery occurs because a wife has allowed a lot of little things to remain unchecked, things like frequent lunches with a man who is not her husband, business trips with a male co-worker, a seemingly harmless flirtation at the gym. Before long, she is caught up in an affair. Committing adultery against God happens the same way. We compromise in little ways, a bit here and a little there, and before we know it, we are ensnared.

Downhill All the Way

Do you know what our sin does to the heart of God? We learn about that as we witness Hosea's broken heart. From Gomer's story, God wants us to see the terrible things that happen when we commit adultery against him and to learn about the slippery slope on which our sin places us. Sometimes sin takes us on a straight course down hill; other times we spiral down. But however we go, the destination is always destruction. God has ordained that; it is a natural law he has placed into effect with all mankind, Christian or not. Paul wrote to the Galatians, "Do not be deceived, God is not mocked; for whatever a man sows, that he will also reap" (Gal. 6:7).

For believers, however, God's intention in allowing us to spiral down is not to bring about our ultimate destruction. Rather, it is an act of his mercy. The fact that sin leads to misery is merciful, because when we are miserable enough we will turn back to him. In fact, repentance from backsliding is guaranteed for believers, because those who are truly saved cannot ever lose their salvation. For Christ's sake, God will not allow us to fall away from him to that extent. Our momentary life on this earth is nothing compared with our life in eternity, and God will go to whatever lengths necessary to preserve us for that.

Think back on the times where you have fallen into sin. Do you recall that it was a happy time? Or is your memory of the occasion one of unhappiness and shame? The apostle Paul wrote, "What fruit did you have then in the things of which you are now ashamed? For the end of those things is death" (Rom. 6:21). The downhill path on which our sin carries us is always similar to Gomer's.[1] Things went pretty well for her at first. Her lovers treated her well; she had an abundance of food, wine, clothes, jewels, and affection. For a season, Gomer's path of sin appeared well paved with pleasure. Hosea and his gloomy prophecies, a life centered on righteousness, seemed boring and dull. "I am so glad to be out from under his roof," Gomer would have thought. "All these lovers—so exhilarating! Now this is real living!" That is the deceitfulness of sin. At first, the idol we set our heart on looks pretty good. As we focus on it, the path of discipleship begins to look unappealing. We wouldn't be tempted by it otherwise!

But before long, the underlying truth begins to emerge. Gomer experienced this when her rich lovers left her for someone new. Mrs. Johnson discovered that her partners in pleasure were only using her. Maybe you are living in a situation that you know is not God's will for you. It might be a relationship you know is wrong or a sinful habit. If that is the case, whatever it is, are you beginning to see the underlying ugliness? Are you getting any glimpses of the misery that awaits you if you continue on this course? When we let obedience slide, little things begin to go wrong, things that spring directly from the sin. That is God's nudging. The Holy Spirit is warning us, sending off little alarm bells meant to tell us that we have gotten off the course of righteousness and that we have set ourselves up for God's discipline.

But if we do not heed those little warnings, worse things begin to happen. Gomer's lavish resources began to shut down, and she found herself struggling for basic necessities. In our case, we are often made to feel that God has gone away and withdrawn his provision and favor from us. Greater problems begin to arise, and in our heart of hearts, we know why. Pastor James Montgomery Boice, in his commentary on Hosea, explains this process well. He wrote, "God is faithful, but one expression of his faithfulness is that when we run away from Him things will not go well. God guarantees that they will not go well. He will scatter our dreams in our faces. You may think that you are going to satisfy yourself by seizing the world and its pleasures, but God will cause them to turn to dust in your mouth, even as you devour them greedily."[2]

Not only do we feel far away from God, but when we persist in a state of backsliding we also tend to isolate ourselves from other believers. We say that we are too busy, or we give some other excuse. But the truth is that we are ashamed, and being around other Christians when we are living in known sin brings us face to face with our conscience. If we are not yet willing to deal with our spiritual adultery, we do not want to get too close to anything or anyone that might convict us.

Taken for a Ride

Before we know it, sooner or later, we discover that the very thing we have been enjoying apart from God is no longer optional. It has enslaved us. Have you experienced that? If so, you probably did not realize you had become enslaved until you tried to get out of the situation or forsake the sin. Smokers often do not realize that they are addicted to nicotine until they try to quit smoking. Those in sinful relationships think, "I've got to end this affair." But when they try to walk out, a broken heart often presents a tremendous pull to go back. God, in speaking to the Israelites through Hosea, said,

> You have plowed wickedness;
> You have reaped iniquity.
> You have eaten the fruit of lies,
> Because you trusted in your own way,
> In the multitude of your mighty men. (Hos. 10:13)

In a nutshell, committing adultery against God happens whenever we give our hearts or our lives to someone or something other than, or even alongside of, him. We can have affairs not only with people but also with things like food, alcohol, our jobs, and our bodies. Those of us who rely on snacking to get us through depression, boredom, or anxiety have created an idol out of food. Those who cannot get through a social situation without a drink are cheating on God with alcohol. Our careers can become idols when we rely on them for personal identity. We make our bodies illicit lovers when we spend an inordinate amount of time focusing on our appearance. Even something good like health can be idolatrous if our concern to be healthy pushes aside our focus on God and his kingdom. He wants us to rely solely on him to get us through everything. When we fail to do so it is an indication that we do not think he is sufficient to meet our needs.

How would you feel if you caught your husband cheating and his explanation to you was, "Honey, I couldn't help it. What do you expect me to do? You're just not enough for me these days. I want more than you can give. Oh, I want you to stick around and be faithful to me. But given your inadequacies, you can't expect me to offer faithfulness in return." As harsh as it sounds, that is what we communicate to God by our sin.

Anything or anyone that captivates our hearts and holds control over our wills is an idol, and idolatry is spiritual adultery. The Bible has much to say about this. Paul wrote, "Do you not know that to whom you present yourselves slaves to obey, you are that one's slaves

whom you obey, whether of sin leading to death, or of obedience leading to righteousness?" (Rom 6:16). From a source that I cannot recall,
I once read a forceful truth that stuck with me: "We are conformed
to that upon which we center our interest and love." That is what
happens when we wake up one day and discover we are enslaved to
our idol. We find that is has tricked us. It is we who were used. Gomer
had to face that fact, if not before, then certainly on the day she stood
naked on the auction block. The smoker with lung cancer, the promis-
cuous woman with a sexually transmitted disease, the runaway parent alienated from her children later in life—they have all found that
to be true.

The Real Scarlet Letter

But at this point, when we are brought to realize fully what our
adultery has done—to God, to others, and to ourselves—God comes
in mercy to restore us to himself. Gomer had been broken in her sin.
She had tasted the bitter consequences, so when Hosea came to lead
her home, she was able to go back there with him. God never stands
over us saying, "Good. I'm glad you're miserable. You deserve whatever you get. Don't expect any help from me!" God doesn't act that
way, any more than Hosea acted that way toward Gomer. God loves
us and longs to have us back with him. The reason he allows us to
suffer when we sin is so that we will want to return to our true Husband. In speaking of wayward Israel, God said through Hosea,

> "I will heal their backsliding,
> I will love them freely,
> for My anger has turned away from him." (Hos. 14:4)

God's love applies not only to Israel but also is as strongly present
for you and me. Are you living in a backslidden condition? If so, listen to God; hear his broken heart. Perhaps even now you are aware
that he is displeased with what you are doing. Little things are going

wrong. If so, it is God acting in mercy to get you to come back before worse things happen.

An important thing to remember is that because God loves us intensely does not mean that he is a pushover. God knows that real love sometimes necessitates standing back and allowing the erring one to suffer great calamity, if, in so doing, he or she will benefit as a result. For this reason God will not stop the consequences of sin if we persist in going our own way. And because he is holy and righteous, he will not allow anything evil ultimately to prosper. If you are living in some way you know is grievous to God, heed the warning inherent in the little calamities you see happening in your life. Doing so will prevent you from worse ones. We can avoid unnecessary pain when we repent and return to our first love.

If you are waking up to find yourself on the auction block, enslaved and unable to free yourself, then turn your heart and mind to God. He has already bid for you and offered the highest price. Hosea paid for Gomer with shekels and barley, but God paid with the life of his son Jesus Christ. By his blood you have been purchased, and your debts have been paid. God will never divorce those who are his through Christ Jesus. You are therefore free to come down off the block, resume the clothing of Christ's righteousness, and return back home with God this day.

16

Mary

Attaching the *Extra* to *Ordinary*

Ordinary Women

"God cannot possibly be asking me to do that," Mary thought. "There must be some mistake. I am a nobody!" Disbelief, panic, and wonder intermingled in Mary when the angel Gabriel came with God's call. Why had she been chosen, a lowly, ordinary woman, for such an important ministry?

When God comes with a great call to ordinary women like Mary and like us, that is often our first reaction. Yet he calls each one of us to glorify him in some unique way. You may be called to several different tasks and ministries at different points in your life, or you may be set apart to accomplish one thing that will take a lifetime. Have you heard God's call on your life? If you are a Christian, you can be sure you have one. Sometimes, like Mary, we are made aware of it rather suddenly. More often, the knowledge of God's leading is established in our mind and heart over a period of time. It is not so much how we discover it that is important but rather how we respond once we do know. Some of us go forward eagerly. Others delay because they are not sure that they really want to go where God is leading them.

And then there are many of us who hesitate, fearing that we are inadequate for the task.

We all admire women who do great things for God, and often we envy them. It seems that God has equipped them with gifts and talents to do things we could never do. We see these women teach the Bible before large groups. We listen to others who host radio programs. Still others dare to leave a comfortable life to serve as missionaries in primitive, isolated places. We are in awe of their courage, wisdom, and godliness, and we wonder how they have been able to become such super-spiritual giants.

In reality, women like that are not spiritual giants. They are ordinary women like you and me. The reason that they are able to do great things for God is that they have become increasingly Christ-oriented rather than self-oriented, something that happens eventually to every woman who receives salvation. In keeping with this truth there are two things necessary for doing great things for God.

The first requirement is purely God's responsibility, a work he undertakes on your behalf, and that is your salvation through the atoning work of Jesus Christ. Salvation is a gift from God, not something that we choose for ourselves. We understand from the apostle Paul that salvation through Christ is a prerequisite for doing God's work. He wrote, "For by grace you have been saved through faith, and that not of yourselves; it is the gift of God, not of works, lest anyone should boast. For we are His workmanship, created in Christ Jesus for good works, which God prepared beforehand that we should walk in them" (Eph. 2:8–10).

The second requirement necessary for doing great things for God is a willingness to serve him in whatever way he calls you to serve. Are you willing to go wherever God asks? Sometimes we are slow to discover his call upon us because we are set on serving him in our own way. We close ourselves off to avenues of service that seem unappealing, trying to convince ourselves and others that we are not gifted to do them. Women who do great things for God are those willing to step out on a limb, even when doing so means possibly relinquishing cherished dreams and personal hopes.

Why Me?

When Mary, who became the mother of Jesus, received her call from God, she faced these very challenges. Mary's call came when she was a young woman, most likely a teenager. At that time she was engaged to marry a man named Joseph. Wedding plans would not have been lavish, her Jewish family being of humble means, but like most brides-to-be she was surely caught up in the excitement of her upcoming marriage. This ordinary young woman, with her deep devotion to God and to her fiancé, had a bright future before her.

It was at this time that the angel Gabriel came to Mary with God's call. He announced, "Rejoice, highly favored one, the Lord is with you; blessed are you among women!" (Luke 1:28). When Mary first heard his words, she was troubled, afraid, and confused. What was the angel telling her? Where was God leading her? Was her well-planned and happy future suddenly turning in a different direction? Her emotions at that moment are understandable. Gabriel said, "Do not be afraid, Mary, for you have found favor with God. And behold, you will conceive in your womb and bring forth a Son, and shall call His name JESUS. He will be called great, and will be called the Son of the Highest; and the Lord God will give Him the throne of His father David. And He will reign over the house of Jacob forever, and of His kingdom there will be no end" (Luke 1:30–33).

What young woman, upon hearing a pronouncement like that, would not sit back in absolute amazement, utterly perplexed? She asked Gabriel a logical question: "How can this be, since I do not know a man?" (Luke 1:34). He explained that she would conceive this child by means of the Holy Spirit; the pregnancy would not come about in a sexual context. Mary did not ask for time to think about it. Rather, she answered Gabriel with wholehearted commitment: "Behold the maidservant of the Lord! Let it be to me according to your word" (Luke 1:38). It is evident from Mary's response that she had already dedicated her life to God's service.

A woman of undeveloped faith would have struggled far more than Mary did, given the obstacles she was about to face. Would her fiancé, Joseph, believe her? Or would he think she was making up a wild story to explain her sudden pregnancy, a story that any rational man would question? In those days, engagements were almost as binding as marriage, and therefore the laws of adultery were equally applicable. The socially acceptable custom, if a woman was found to have been unfaithful during the engagement, was for the man to break it off. Therefore, Mary knew that there was this great risk in accepting God's call.

Not only would Joseph perhaps disbelieve her, but also her friends and family. She might be put out of the synagogue in shame and disgrace! Who would ever marry her after something like this? She would be a marked woman for the rest of her life, a life that had looked so promising. But God held first place in Mary's heart, and she trusted him to take care of her, which he did.

And indeed Joseph did not want to continue the engagement when he found out that Mary was pregnant, yet here we discover how God provided for what he guided. We read, "But while he thought about these things, behold, an angel of the Lord appeared to him in a dream, saying, 'Joseph, son of David, do not be afraid to take to you Mary your wife, for that which is conceived in her is of the Holy Spirit.' . . . Then Joseph, being aroused from sleep, did as the angel of the Lord commanded him and took to him his wife, and did not know her till she had brought forth her firstborn Son. And he called His name JESUS" (Matt. 1:20, 24–25).

A Call to Joy

As Mary stepped out in faith in response to God's call, she ran headlong into the greatest blessing that comes to all who do this. She was filled with a joy so overflowing that she could hardly contain it. Such joy comes to all those who realize they have been chosen by God for a unique work, a means of glorifying him in a way no one else can do in quite the same manner. With that realization comes an awesome sense of humility that asks, "God, why me? Who am I that you should call me for this?" Even when the call involves great suffering, there is a sense of wonder that God chooses us for the task of bringing him glory in it. Such joy, therefore, springs from humility, gratitude, wonder, and the knowledge that we are bound up in the arms of his protective love as we go forward in what he has asked us to do.

That blessing of joy often comes soon after we commit to the course God has called us to and we have started on our way. It is not reserved for after we have completed the job. I believe God brings such joy early for many reasons, particularly to confirm to us that we are on the right track. God also gives us joy so that we may know that he delights in our desire to serve him. Additionally, spiritual joy keeps us focused on him. Somewhere along the path of service we will encounter troubles and perplexities of one sort or another; when that happens, the memory of those periods of great joy will sustain us.

Something else we learn from Mary about the joy that accompanies serving God is that an attitude of humility is necessary for experiencing it. We find this attitude in Mary's song of praise recorded in Luke 1:46–55.[1] In it Mary lists all the reasons why she is filled with the joy of the Lord. She rejoices that he has done great things for her and that he has shown her his strength. Not only was she, a young girl from a poor Jewish family, the chosen virgin to bear the long-awaited Savior of her people, but also God had worked it so that Joseph was accepting of the situation and married her as planned. She found what we all find when we risk the loss of something for God, namely, that he will take care of everything that obedience might cost us. If we lose something, he will ensure that we gain something even better. Mary exclaimed, "My soul magnifies the Lord, and my spirit has rejoiced in God my Savior. For He has regarded the lowly state of His maidservant; for behold, henceforth all generations will call me blessed" (Luke 1:46–48).

You can see the sense of wonder and awe that Mary felt at being chosen to serve God, accompanied by deep humility. Such humility deepened Mary's commitment, her zeal, and her love, enabling her to serve God as he had asked. God knew that these qualities—humility, gratitude, joy, and commitment—were important prerequisites for Mary's calling, because becoming the mother of the human Jesus proved not only to be an awesome responsibility; it also was to bring her much pain.

No Primrose Paths

Mary was given an inkling of this pain not long after Jesus was born. She and Joseph came to the temple to present the child to God and to have him circumcised, customs observed by devout Jews eight days after the birth. A man named Simeon presided over the circumcision, and afterward he said to Mary, "Behold, this Child is destined for the fall and rising of many in Israel, and for a sign which will be spoken against (yes, a sword will pierce through your own soul also), that the thoughts of many hearts may be revealed" (Luke 2:34–35).

If you know the story of Jesus' life, you know that Simeon's words came true. Mary's unique call lasted for the thirty-three years that she mothered him, beginning with his birth on the hard ground of a stable and ending with his death on the cross, a torturous death that she witnessed. Those of you who are mothers know that even the thought of seeing your child die is more than you can bear to think of. But God equipped Mary to bear it, and she did.

Mary also had to deal with the more typical aspects of parenting. An incident from Jesus' boyhood is recorded in Luke. When he was twelve years old, Jesus and his parents went up to Jerusalem for the Feast of the Passover. Afterwards, a full day into the return journey home, Mary and Joseph discovered that the young Jesus was missing. Back then, people traveled in large caravans and it was customary for the men to travel together behind the women and children. If that were the case here, it is likely that each parent believed Jesus to be in the care of the other, or they may have believed he was with his friends or other relatives somewhere within the caravan. Regardless of what led to the mix-up, Mary and Joseph were sick with worry when they discovered Jesus missing.

After three frantic days of searching, they found him in Jerusalem. They came upon their son in the temple where he was engrossed in conversation with many learned scholars. If you are a parent who has found your child safe and oblivious to your fear of potential catastrophe, you know that such fear often gives way to extreme annoyance. That is what Mary felt. She said, "Son, why have You done this to us? Look, Your father and I have sought You anxiously" (Luke 2:48). Rather than hanging his head with remorse, Jesus said, "Why did you seek Me? Did you not know that I must be about My Father's business?" (Luke 2:49).

Jesus was not being disrespectful; he was reminding Mary that his divinity, his union with God, and the purpose for which he had come to earth must supersede any other consideration. Therefore, Mary should not expect to receive from him the normal deference a son paid his mother if it interfered with his greater purpose. His answer to her makes that clear. Yet, since Jesus was without fault in every way, he was an obedient son, so he got up and went home with his parents.

Very likely another constant difficulty for Mary was her knowledge that he was as divine as he was human. No one but Mary will ever know the dilemmas of parenting such a son. We cannot imagine how we would train up a child who was God! But God provided her with all she needed for such an awesome responsibility as each new need arose. Perplexities such as Mary faced are the kinds of concerns that we anticipate about our calling and that make us say, "God, I can't do it. Please choose someone else for that particular task." It takes faith to go forward into all the unknowns. God rarely reveals ahead of time exactly how he will provide for us; rather, he shows us as the need arises so we will depend on him every step of the way.

Mary also faced temptation to misuse her special calling, temptation that Jesus used, on one occasion, to perform his first miracle. Jesus, his disciples, and Mary were attending a wedding in Cana, and during the festivities all the wine had been consumed. Mary knew that Jesus could do something about that, so she told him of the quandary. Even though Jesus did what Mary wished, he made it clear that, although she was his mother, she had no special claim on his divinity. He said to her, gently but firmly, "Woman, what does your concern have to do with Me? My hour has not yet come" (John 2:4). How humbling for a mother—to be rebuked by her son!

The last three years of Jesus' earthly life were assuredly the most difficult in Mary's special calling. Those were the years of Jesus' public ministry, the years when he became famous for his miracles and his teaching. He also became less and less popular as he spread the truth of God's kingdom throughout the land. Eventually the governing authorities sought to stop him by using whatever tactics were necessary. Though the Bible does not mention this, there is no doubt that, as the mother of this reputed troublemaker, Mary was not exempt from persecution. She was likely scorned by longtime friends because they were either embarrassed or afraid. Perhaps Mary was even threatened with imprisonment. Additionally, no mention is made of her husband after the incident in the temple with the twelve-year-old Jesus; it is widely assumed that he died before Jesus reached adulthood. If that is the case, Mary witnessed the growing hostility against her son without Joseph's comfort. Nevertheless, she remained faithful to what God had called her to do even when the path was treacherous.

God never promises freedom from trouble when he calls us to something. What he does promise is to be with us through it. Sometimes suffering is part of the calling, not just a by-product of it. This is true of those who are called to endure a long illness or other physical malady. Joni Earickson Tada, author and Christian radio host, is an example. When still a young woman, Joni became permanently paralyzed from the neck down in a diving accident. Out of her paralysis has sprung a ministry of international proportions, a ministry that most likely would not have occurred apart from the accident. Joni, at a young age, was called to serve God through physical suffering. All along the way she has known God's provision for each of her needs and, quite obviously, great personal fulfillment as well.

The most agonizing period of Mary's calling as the mother of Jesus came at the end of her son's life. Knowing him to be innocent of the crimes with which he was charged, she nevertheless witnessed much of his trials, his torture, and his cruel execution—images that would scar her memory for life. No other mother in all of history has had an experience quite like it. But this too was tied up with God's calling, and God provided for her in her darkest hour. As she watched, helpless and brokenhearted while her son hung torn and bleeding on the cross, the crowd jeering at him, at his followers, and likely at her, God came to comfort her in her agony. The provision came through Jesus during his dying moments.

It was recorded, "Now there stood by the cross of Jesus His mother, and His mother's sister, Mary the wife of Clopas, and Mary Magdalene. When Jesus therefore saw His mother, and the disciple whom He loved standing by, He said to His mother, 'Woman, behold your son!' Then He said to the disciple, 'Behold your mother!' And from that hour that disciple took her to his own home" (John 19:25–27). Jesus united his grief-stricken mother with one of his closest friends for the comfort of both. John would receive comfort from Mary, and she in turn would have a foster son to assuage her pain.

A Cost Worth Paying

Although Mary experienced suffering as she lived out her calling, she knew more joy than sorrow as a result. Not only was she infused with overwhelming, supernatural joy as she began her mission; she also experienced the privilege of living daily life in the presence of Jesus Christ. And finally, the words Mary sang in her song of praise have come true, "For behold, henceforth all generations will call me blessed" (Luke 1:48). She was an ordinary woman like you and me, yet her commitment to her calling brought her blessings of eternal value.

From Mary we see that if we follow God wherever he leads, even when it requires personal sacrifice, we will never look back in regret. Women like Mary, who do great things for God, who find and live out their personal calling (or callings) to the fullest, are often required to relinquish their own way. But there is always an exciting discovery prepared for those who go forward willingly, and that is the discovery of blessings beyond their greatest expectations, unexpected blessings both spiritual and temporal. Jesus said, "Assuredly, I say to you, there is no one who has left house or brothers or sisters or father or mother or wife or children or lands, for My sake and the gospel's, who shall not receive a hundredfold now in this time—houses and brothers and sisters and mothers and children and lands, with persecutions—and in the age to come, eternal life" (Mark 10:29–30).

Perhaps you sense that God is calling you to a path that will take you away from your previously set goals. If so, remember how God provided for Mary when he came to call her in the midst of her wedding plans. With that in mind, accept the challenge to go forward with anticipation of all God will do in and through your life. If you step out in faith and take those risks, you will surely do great things for God.

An important thing to keep in mind, however, is that most of us are not called to greatness, even though we are called to do great things. Often God means to use us for his glory in the most ordinary of circumstances. Although less visible, such work is no less glorifying to God. In fact, he is often most glorified by those who are faithful in the little things of day-to-day life. So if you are called to serve God through a career in accounting, then that is how you can most honor him and find the greatest fulfillment. If he has called you to motherhood, then how you rear your children can bring him glory for generations to come.

Whether it is to be found in the commonplace or in specific, unusual circumstances, if you confess Jesus Christ, God has a calling for you. If you are serious about living for him, as Mary was, and if you are willing to commit yourself to whatever and wherever he may take you, there are great blessings in store for you. With such great promises attached, why hold back? Theologian J. I. Packer addressed this question in his book *Knowing God*. He wrote, "Have you been holding back from a risky, costly course to which you know in your heart God has called you? Hold back no longer. Your God is faithful to you, and adequate for you. You will never need more than he can supply, and what he supplies, both materially and spiritually, will always be enough for the present."[2]

Will you take that risk? If you are his daughter, and if you are willing to do whatever he asks you to do for him, you can accomplish great things for God, just as the women whom you admire do. It is that simple.

17

Anna

Far from Over

Bruised Reeds

The bright postcard was the first thing Nancy spotted as she sorted through her mail. It announced of the upcoming church picnic, an annual event she had enjoyed for years. But not this year. For years Nancy and Ed had relished the full day of lighthearted fun with friends from church, but Ed was gone now.

Last week the pastor's wife had paid a call on Nancy and had encouraged her to get out again. "Ed died nine months ago, Nancy," she had said. "It's time for you to get involved with people again."

"I don't fit anymore!" Nancy had replied. "Ed and I did all those things together. I don't know how to go out and do them alone. We were a couple for so many years, and almost everything we did was with other couples. They won't want me by myself. I'll just be Ed's widow, a fifth wheel at every function. I'm afraid that people will only include me out of pity!"

"That's not true, Nancy," the pastor's wife had countered. "You weren't a complete person because you had Ed, and you're not merely half a person now that he's gone. People want you just for you. You're an important part of our church."

Nancy wasn't convinced. Nor did she have the desire to force herself back out there as a single woman. She'd been part of a couple for decades, and facing the world alone now was too hard. Staying at home felt safe regardless of the loneliness.

Many women can empathize with Nancy. At first there is the intense grief over the loss of a spouse, and once that abates somewhat, there is the inevitable fear and anxiety of resuming a normal life. Women who have been married for many decades are scared of going back out into the world without the protection of their husbands. The difficulty is even more intense for women whose spouses have abandoned them. Those women not only must deal with grief and starting over again, but they also have the horrors of rejection and humiliation to contend with and the stigma of divorce. Whether widowed or divorced, many of them have no desire to start over. It all feels too overwhelming.

If you find yourself in this situation, the story of Anna holds out hope, not only for how to begin living again but also for how to find great joy in doing so. We learn about Anna in the Gospel of Luke, where her story is told in only three verses. On the eighth day of Jesus' life, his parents, Mary and Joseph, brought him to the temple to be circumcised. Anna happened to come into the temple at that time, and she saw the baby Jesus and knew immediately that he was the long-awaited Messiah. Luke tells us:

> Now there was one, Anna, a prophetess, the daughter of Phanuel, of the tribe of Asher. She was of a great age, and had lived with a husband seven years from her virginity; and this woman was a widow of about eighty-four years, who did not depart from the temple, but served God with fastings and prayers night and day. And coming in that instant she gave thanks to the Lord, and spoke of Him to all those who looked for redemption in Jerusalem. (Luke 2:36–38)

Anna was a widow and had lived the majority of her life without her mate. In fact, she was married for only seven years before her husband died, leaving her to face a solitary life for many decades. But Anna belonged to God, and to him she turned for comfort and help in establishing a life without her husband. As we can see from her story, God helped Anna to focus her life in the temple, and it is there that she found everything she needed. Anna knew a great truth about life, and that is, if we have God, we have everything we need. Anna lived in constant fellowship with God and surrounded herself with his people. Through doing so, she lived a purposeful, rewarding life in spite of losing her husband.

Perhaps at this point you do not find Anna's life encouraging. You may be thinking, "What sort of a life is that, spending every moment in church praying and fasting? What about the need for people in my life?" Or you may be thinking that Anna's lifestyle isn't practical in today's world. "Even if I wanted to," you may say, "how could I spend all my time in church? There are financial considerations, a house to maintain, and dozens of other daily concerns." This is true; making a literal application from Anna's life might not help you much. There are many practical concerns with which you must necessarily be occupied. Yet there are a few crucial aspects of Anna's approach to widowhood upon which you can establish your life if you find yourself alone.

Family Ties

The first is the fact that Anna surrounded herself with others who worshiped God. If you are a Christian woman, alone without a spouse, you can still experience true companionship with other believers. In fact, it is God's will for you to do so. God never intended for his people to live in isolation. He desires that we live in community with one another. That is how we grow, and it is the means God has provided to meet many of our needs. If you pray for Christian companionship, you can be sure that God will give it to you. His Word says,

> A father of the fatherless, a defender of widows,
> Is God in His holy habitation.
> God sets the solitary in families;
> He brings out those who are bound into prosperity;
> But the rebellious dwell in a dry land. (Ps. 68:5–6)

Are you alone? Do you have no family? God promises to give you one with his people, and he provides it through the local church. It is crucial that you find and become a member of a God-worshiping, Bible-believing church, a local gathering of fellow believers. That is one of the most important aspects of finding meaning and fulfillment in the Christian life. It is so important that if you do not live near a church that adheres to God's Word, you should change your life so that you can do so. Just as marriage is a spiritual union, so is our union with all other believers. Through our union with Christ, we are all united to one another through him. We are more closely tied to other believers than we are to blood relatives outside the faith.

I belong to a large urban church that draws its members from the city and its suburbs. Yet over time I have discovered that those who benefit most from belonging to this church are those who live closest to it. Many people live within a few blocks of the church, and they spend time together on a weekly basis involved in ministry activities, eating meals together, and shouldering one another's burdens. For those of us who have structured our lives around the church and its members, it has become a true family. Missing out on such fellowship happens when believers choose to reside far apart from each other, opting for a nicer house or a bigger back yard instead of settling for something on a smaller scale nearer to their church. They have misunderstood the priorities of the Christian life, and that has left them destitute.

So if you are alone and lonely, you will find your remedy by affixing yourself firmly into a community of fellow believers. Perhaps you are newly on your own, and taking the first steps to get involved seems frightening and overwhelming. God knows that, and he will help you to take those steps. Remember, it is his will to bless you in that way, so you can be confident that your path will be smoothed out as you move forward. Anna found a full and rich life in the Jewish temple because others who worshiped God were there too. How much more can we through our union with one another in Christ!

Father, Husband, and Friend

Yet even more fulfilling than the company of other believers is our personal fellowship with God. Have you found him to be comforter, friend, and husband, as well as Lord? Anna surely did; otherwise she would not have spent the majority of her time in prayer and fasting. She was not compelled to do that. I think many of us see fellowship with God as a sort of consolation when people are missing from our lives. We turn to him only when we have no one else. When we think that way, we are missing out on enjoying the best relationship we will ever have. The Westminster Shorter Catechism asks, "What is the chief end of man?" to which the answer is "Man's chief end is to glorify God, and to enjoy him forever." Anna knew her chief end. Not only did she glorify him in how she lived her life, but also she knew the joy of an intimate relationship.

Many of us miss out on coming to know the great joy to be found in God because we are not looking to him for it. Oh, we want God, but we also want other things in equal if not greater measure. Longing for a mate and companionship are not wrong desires. God designed us that way. We find ourselves miserable, however, when we determine that we need those things in order to be happy.

Biblical counselor David Powlison brings this truth to light where he writes, "The Christian life is a great paradox. Those who die to self, find self. Those who die to their cravings will receive many times as much in this age, and in the age to come, eternal life (Luke 18:29–30). If I crave happiness, I will receive misery. If I crave to be loved, I will receive rejection. If I crave significance, I will receive futility. If I crave control, I will receive chaos. If I crave reputation, I will receive humiliation. But if I long for God and his wisdom, I will receive God and his wisdom. Along the way, sooner or later, I will also receive happiness, love, meaning, order, and glory."[1]

No one knows us better, has more compassion for our heartbreak and sorrows, and more completely offers the means of healing than God does. He is there to listen constantly, and he is there in his Word to speak to you at any time. He also knows the best way for each of us individually to get up and get on with living when our world has turned upside down.

All Things New

Are you struggling to find a sense of meaning and purpose now that your mate is gone? Anna found it by pouring her life out in service to God. Then, after she had seen Jesus in the temple, she went about proclaiming that the Savior had come, spreading the good news of salvation in Jerusalem. What greater purpose could there be? Regardless of whether or not you are alone, God wants to use you for his glory and if you are willing, he will place you in an arena of service for his kingdom to which you are uniquely suited.

One of the benefits of being alone is the freedom you have to serve God unhindered. Whether you have never married, are widowed or are divorced, the fact that you are on your own is a great privilege, an honor that God does not bestow on everyone. Those who are caught up in the concerns of family life have less time to devote to God and his work. If you have no mate at present, it is because God has set you apart to be more available for him. Married women, especially those rearing children, are taken up with the care of others most hours of every day. One of their greatest struggles is finding any time when they can slip off for a few minutes of solitude with God. Those without a family are blessed with an abundance of discretionary time, hours to devote to prayer, reading God's Word, and serving him in a variety of ways alongside like-minded believers. This is a special blessing.

The apostle Paul stressed this to those who were unmarried or widowed in the early church at Corinth. He wrote,

But she who is married cares about the things of the world—
how she may please her husband. And this I say for your own
profit, not that I may put a leash on you, but for what is proper,
and that you may serve the Lord without distraction. . . . A
wife is bound by law as long as her husband lives; but if her
husband dies, she is at liberty to be married to whom she
wishes, only in the Lord. But she is happier if she remains as
she is, according to my judgment—and I think I have the
Spirit of God. (1 Cor. 7:34–35, 39–40)

Happier if we remain without a spouse? Yes, according to the apostle Paul. Although he was writing to believers who were living under
threat of persecution and his words were therefore intended for those
who needed to be easily mobile and unencumbered, the principle still
applies to believers. The principle is that those without a mate are
freer to spend time enjoying and glorifying God.

Have you found that for yourself? If not, why not set your heart to
seek your all in him? If you feel that you are not able to do that, you
can begin by asking God to beget in your heart a passionate zeal to
discover for yourself that he is all he promises to be. If you do, you
will find what the Psalmist Asaph found that caused him to write,

Whom have I in heaven but You?
And there is none upon earth that I desire besides You.
My flesh and my heart fail;
But God is the strength of my heart and my portion forever.
(Ps. 73:25–26)

18

Mary Magdalene
Dearly Beloved

"Lonely Female Seeks Love . . ."

There is nothing quite like the emotional intensity of being in love. The visceral feelings and obsessive thoughts of such love push less impassioned loves into obscurity. Many women have known passionate love like that, and just as many others, including women who are happily married, have never experienced it. Love like that is not necessary for happiness, contrary to contemporary belief. Our culture is permeated with the conviction that being in love is the pinnacle of life, that without it we are doomed to a life of mediocrity and incapable of developing true depth of character. Its sexual link also contributes to that, because today many people believe a person without a sexual relationship is unenlightened. We are fed the "true love" propaganda everywhere we turn, in the books we read, on television, and by well meaning friends.

An example of such propaganda arrived in my mailbox this week, a catalog offering evening classes at a local college. As I perused the latest course listing, I came across a new class called Single Solutions. The course was described as follows: "This interactive class will focus on solutions to living life to the fullest as a single person. We will look into, but not be limited by, the topics of holiday dread, loneliness, friendship, meeting people, and finding meaning in your life when you're not currently partnered."

I find that sad because there are so many lost people who do not know the love and fulfillment found in a relationship with Jesus Christ. I also find it frustrating that so many women do not yet know that the deepest, most intimate relationship they will ever have is with Jesus. Contributing to that lack of knowledge is the fact that evangelicals have so blended with the surrounding culture that the world's thinking, its agenda, and its fears have derailed that truth. It is no wonder that women, even Christian women, feel they are missing something if they do not have a great love, one that culminates in physical passion and intimacy.

What sort of relationship do you have with Jesus? Do you love him in a way that involves your emotions and your actions? I think many of us are troubled about that. We see a few people who display great passion for Jesus. We hear it in their singing and in their conversation; they even glow when they talk about him, just like a woman in love. We look at that and wonder, What's wrong with me? Why is my heart so cold? Then we conclude that such people are wired differently from us.

Our love for Jesus is based on faith first and then on intellect; however, it should be characterized by an emotional element as well. Yet all too often, it seems to remain more intellectual than heartfelt. We know what Jesus did for us, we believe, and we are grateful. Nevertheless there is a lack of passion, the kind of love that grips every part of our being. I have long wished for a heart to refrain from sin out of love for God, but all too often I am motivated to obedience by fear of sin's consequences instead. We hunger to love passionately, and when we do not find it within ourselves toward Christ, it tends to reinforce the world's premise of true love all the more.

A Holy Obsession

The story of Mary Magdalene is a story for all who hunger for true love, for those who long for a deep, visceral, all-consuming passion that never disappoints, or fades, or grows disillusioned. From Mary Magdalene we learn that it is possible to experience that kind of love for Jesus Christ and that Jesus longs to have that sort of relationship with each one of us.

How did Mary come to love Jesus so deeply? Mary was a woman from the town of Magdala, which is how the Bible distinguishes her from the other Marys in the New Testament. Before she met Jesus, her life was miserable. Mary lived life tormented by seven demons. The Bible does not tell us specifically how the demons afflicted her, whether they affected her body or her mind, but whatever the manifestation was, it would have robbed her of the ability to live in peace. But Mary's demon possession was the vehicle God used to bring about her relationship with Jesus. Perhaps he saw her overtaken by the powers of evil one day and reached out his hand to heal her. Or perhaps she was brought to him for healing by someone else. The point is that without this horrible affliction, Mary Magdalene may never have come in close personal contact with Jesus. Her relationship with him began from the moment he delivered her, and from that point on she joined with his band of close followers.

Mary's love was born out of gratitude. If Jesus had not looked favorably upon her and reached out to save her, she would have been doomed to a life of misery. But afterward she was free to really live, to experience the normal life of a healthy woman. All because of Jesus, she could wake up each day in her right mind without the fear that evil beyond her control would hold her imprisoned. Mary had been powerless to free herself. How could she help but love the one who had done this for her!

That is how true love for Jesus begins for us, too. We are powerless to save ourselves, to free ourselves of our demons, the sin that hardens our hearts and ruins our lives. We are never saved because we decide we want to be. Nor are we saved by getting our act together or doing good things. We can enter into the joy of fellowship with Jesus only because he reaches out to pluck us from the power of Satan and our sin. Jesus, in speaking to the apostles, said, "You did not choose Me, but I chose you and appointed you that you should go and bear fruit, and that your fruit should remain, that whatever you ask the Father in My name He may give you" (John 15:16). All the benefits of salvation come to us because God determined to give them to us, and it is through Jesus Christ that those benefits are manifest. "We love Him because He first loved us" (1 John 4:19). That is why Mary first loved him so passionately.

What did Mary do with her newfound freedom? Rather than returning to her hometown of Magdala, she joined Jesus and his band of followers as they moved around Galilee. In addition to Mary, there were a number of women attached to the group, and everyone within the group benefited from the unique skills the women brought to them. The Bible tell us nothing of Mary's past or of her family, yet we know she must have been a woman of independent means since she helped to support the disciples by contributing her possessions (Luke 8:1–3).

Intimacy Required

Mary's love for Jesus was born out of gratitude, but it grew and deepened as a result of living daily in his presence. Think about the people you love most. Aren't they the ones with whom you spend the most time and in whom you invest the most energy? That is how love for Jesus grows, too. Our love for him will not deepen without that. It is through close, intimate, one-on-one communion with another that the deepest relationships are established. Did you come to love your husband merely by spending time with his friends, finding out about him from them? Of course not! Real love developed as you interacted with him personally.

It is no different with love for Jesus. Deep love will not come merely by attending worship service on Sunday, participating in a small-group Bible study, or reading books about him. All those things give us a sound understanding of who he is, which is necessary for real love, but also of vital importance is setting apart time to be alone with him. During such times the Holy Spirit is at work applying the truth of Jesus Christ, as revealed in Scripture, to our hearts. The solitary moments are also those when we are most prone to pour out our hearts in prayer, revealing our deepest yearnings and true selves. It is through such exposure of ourselves to Jesus, and of him to us, that love flourishes intellectually, emotionally, and spiritually.

Mary loved Jesus because she revolved each day around him. She talked with him in the mornings, listened and observed his ways throughout the day, shared his meals, and served his needs. Giving ourselves to another also increases love. Those we love most are usually those to whom we have devoted our energy and time. That was Mary's experience; it can also be ours, to an even greater degree. Although Mary had Jesus beside her, we actually have him in us by means of the Holy Spirit. Through the Spirit, Jesus resides in, not merely alongside of, every believer.

A friend of mine, Alexis, was once deeply in love with a man, so deeply that her intensity scared him off. During the heyday of the relationship, I recall her saying to me once, "I just want to swallow him whole." Her desire and attempt to be fused with this man smothered him, and as for Alexis, she became immensely frustrated. What she did not realize was that the depth of love she was craving to give and receive can be found only in a relationship with Jesus. It is not possible between human beings. God created us with the capacity to long for love like that, and then he went on to provide us with the means for its fulfillment by giving us Jesus. When we look elsewhere, we are bound to be disappointed.

Mary seemed to have no such conflict. She had found her love, and she poured her heart there, and by so doing, she found what we will too; namely, that Jesus is the one person who will never be smothered by our yearning. He will never be bored, unloving, inconsiderate, or unfaithful. We cannot possibly love Jesus too much. On the contrary, as we pour ourselves into such love, we will find that our desire to love and be loved is met completely.

Mary's love went so deep that she refused to leave Jesus at the end of his life, even when many disciples had fled in fear. That is because true love cannot abandon the object of its affection, even at peril of life and limb. During the course of Jesus' arrest and trial, those who had followed him faithfully during the preceding three years of his ministry now stood in danger of persecution as well. Jesus' reputation as a troublemaker, an insurrectionist, and a heretic had grown steadily to the point where the governing authorities perceived him as a threat to their established ways of life and religion. The leaders were well aware of this eclectic group of disciples made up of fisherman, tax collectors, sickly people, and independent women. Upstarts, all of them, the authorities believed, and the only way to stop them was to stop their leader. The disciples were far from safe, however, because at any time during Jesus' arrest and trial, any or all of them could easily have been arrested and put to death as well. Mary was not oblivious to such danger, but her love for Jesus pushed out consideration for her safety.

Realities of Love: Sacrifice and Sorrow

Mary's love was as deep as that of devoted parents toward their children. Loving parents are willing to sacrifice anything and everything to rescue a troubled child, and to experience great personal sacrifice so that their children may benefit. Mary's love was also like the love of a sister who unhesitatingly donates a kidney to get her brother off of dialysis. It is the kind of love that agonizes when the beloved one is suffering.

The Gospels tell us that Mary was among those who witnessed Jesus' execution. She saw her Savior, dearest friend, and most intimate companion spat upon, beaten, and ridiculed. She saw him nailed to a cross and raised up into the air to slowly suffocate. She heard him cry out in the agony of abandonment by his Father. She heard him, in the extremity of his pain, reach down to provide for his grieving mother and his favored disciple, John. She saw a soldier stab him in his side, further desecrating the body of the one she loved so much.

When Joseph of Arimathea was given permission to take Jesus and bury him, Mary was among the women who followed along to witness the burial. As Joseph wrapped Jesus' body in linen and laid it in the tomb, the women observed how and where he was laid so that they could come back after the Sabbath and anoint the body with oil and spices, a final act of love. The day after the Sabbath, before dawn, Mary and a few other women crept through the dark garden toward the tomb, but as they approached, they saw that the stone covering the entrance had been rolled away. The body of Jesus was gone! Mary, in utter dismay, turned and ran out of the garden, stumbling upon Peter and John as she fled. She said to them, "They have taken away the Lord out of the tomb, and we do not know where they have laid Him" (John 20:2).

Together they ran back to the garden. Peter and John peered inside and saw the linen cloths lying on the floor of the tomb, and the handkerchief that had been wrapped around Jesus' head had been neatly folded and laid beside the cloths. If someone had come in to steal the body or violate the grave, why were the grave clothes in such neat order? The disciples were perplexed. Even though Jesus had told them all what would happen—his crucifixion, his burial, and his subsequent resurrection—they still did not realize what was indicated by the missing body. So John, Peter, and the others returned to their homes. All except Mary.

John's Gospel tells us that after the others had left, she remained behind, standing outside the tomb weeping. She couldn't go home! How could she possibly leave and go about her business until Jesus was found? She felt as a mother feels at midnight when her teenager is still out somewhere, two hours past curfew. She cannot go to bed. She cannot watch television or read a book with any degree of concentration. Likewise, in desperation Mary peered once again into the tomb, and much to her surprise she saw two angels sitting inside. They asked her why she was weeping, and she replied, "Because they have taken away my Lord, and I do not know where they have laid Him" (John 20:13).

Notice how she refers to Jesus as "my" Lord. When we refer to someone as ours—"my child," "my husband," "my friend"—we are implying personal ownership and possession. True love always has this element of possessiveness. It indicates a sense of belonging, an emotional and spiritual ownership. There is that element of love in Jesus toward all those whom he loves. Mary knew she belonged to Jesus, and he belonged to her. That is how Jesus wants us to feel, and as our relationship with him deepens, so will that godly possessiveness.

After Mary had spoken with the angels, she turned around and saw someone else standing beside her. It was Jesus, but she did not recognize him. He asked her, "Woman, why are you weeping? Whom are you seeking?" (John 20:15). If you recall, addressing a female as "woman" was not an unkind form of address. It was the customary way that Jesus addressed the women he knew, including his mother, and it was respectful. As Mary answered this man standing next to her beside the tomb, she thought he was merely the gardener. So she said to him, " 'Sir, if you have carried Him away, tell me where you have laid Him, and I will take Him away.' Jesus said to her, 'Mary!' She turned and said to Him, 'Rabboni!' (which is to say, Teacher)" (John 20:15–16).

A Matter of Give and Take

It was in that way that Mary became the first of his devoted followers to whom Jesus appeared. Mark's Gospel reports, "Now when He rose early on the first day of the week, He appeared first to Mary Magdalene, out of whom He had cast seven demons. She went and told those who had been with Him, as they mourned and wept" (Mark 16:9–10). The Bible does not tell us why he appeared to Mary before the others, but we can be sure that he knew that Mary's great love for him was causing her tremendous emotional suffering, and he wanted to ease that. Because she saw him, Mary was blessed with comfort and reassurance. In light of this story, we find that Mary is historical proof that Jesus reveals himself to those who love and seek him. That is as great a blessing for us as it was for Mary. Since Jesus is light, joy, peace, freedom, and love, those who see him are, therefore, able to bask in that light, joy, peace, freedom, and love, and participate in the benefits of every other trait that characterizes him.

The fact that Jesus revealed himself first to Mary shows us how much he values being loved so passionately. Intellectual knowledge is insufficient because there is no passion in it. Pure emotion is inadequate, because it stems from impulse rather than from a true knowledge of who he is. Knowledge is necessary in order to have a sound basis for giving our love. Our emotions are our response to what we have learned. That is why true love for Jesus includes our minds, our wills, and our emotions—every part of us. Mary loved Jesus that way, and in turn she experienced the joy of his love.

On Your Doorstep

Do you have a clearer picture of what is available for you now? Do you realize that you do not have to look any farther or wait any longer for true love? If you are yearning to give yourself to someone who will love you intimately in return, you can have that with Jesus Christ, and you can begin building that deep relationship this day. We have learned from Mary Magdalene how to begin.

If you are still skeptical about being able to experience love of the deepest sort for Jesus, go back and start where Mary did. Think back on the demons he has cast out of you. Has he freed you from impossibly difficult circumstances or from a bad relationship? Perhaps he has delivered you from an addiction or other besetting sin from which you knew you could never free yourself. Remember how Mary's love began—with gratitude. Pray for a heart overflowing with thanks, because even that is not something we can manufacture on our own.

Then, like Mary, give him your life. Live each day in fellowship with him through prayer, meditating on his Word, worshiping him in church, and surrounding yourself with his people as much as possible. Frequently the emotions of love follow along after the actions we take to build it. Too often today we equate love with its emotional by-product. That is an unfortunate misconception, because emotion never holds the seeds of true love.

That truth applies to love for God and love for one another. I learned that some years ago from my grandmother. During the 1920s, my grandmother had two suitors. One was a charming and handsome military officer, an exciting man for whom my grandmother felt great attraction, what we call chemistry. The other suitor was not nearly so debonair or sophisticated. He was a young attorney set up to practice law in his father's firm, a man destined to live his life in the town of his birth, a steady, reliable, dependable man yet one much less likely to stir up the passions of a young and popular woman. Although she was in love with the West Point officer, my grandmother chose to marry the attorney, my grandfather, a man whom she admired but for whom she felt no great passion. She based her choice on character rather than charm, on reputation rather than starry-eyed rapture—because she believed that in the long run she was setting her life on a wiser course. Within one year of marrying my grandfather, as his character was revealed day to day in life's changes and events, she fell deeply in love with him with a love that endured until his death sixty-three years later.

The same thing that happened to my grandmother will happen to us as we give ourselves to Jesus Christ. The more time you spend with him, the more you get to know him as he is; and as you see what tender care and interest he takes in your welfare, you cannot help but love him as Mary Magdalene did. And when you do, you will discover that it is the most satisfying love you'll ever know.

19

Martha

A Colorful Personality

Shaded Viewpoints

"I think you are making a big mistake co-signing that loan for Valery. You are putting your credit at risk," Amanda warned.

"I know," Susan replied, "But she really needs help. She needs a car, plus she has all those school loans to pay back."

"She's thirty-five years old!" Amanda argued. "And you have school loans too! She should find a way to stand on her own two feet at her age."

"You're so black and white about things," Susan defended herself. "Not everything is so cut and dried. There is a lot of gray in this situation. You're way too critical of Valery!"

Would you classify yourself as a black-and-white woman like Amanda? Or are you gray like Susan? Most of us are either one or the other. A black-and-white woman makes quick decisions about almost everything, from what to wear in the morning to assessing the character of other people. Gray women cringe at the behavior of women who have a black-and-white temperament. A gray woman believes that an investment of time and thought offers a better guarantee of a good and accurate outcome. She carefully weighs and considers all the nuances of a given situation in order to avoid a wrong decision. A woman with a gray temperament is often quick to excuse the faults of others, preferring to err on the side of compassion.

If you have no trouble identifying yourself as fitting into one category or the other, you are probably black and white! In either case, God has made you the way you are. Whether black and white or gray, the strengths of your personality will prove to be a blessing to yourself and to others, whereas God will use your weaknesses to teach you many things.

The Good and the Bad about Martha

The New Testament gives us a strong example of a black-and-white woman, a woman who was prone to snap judgments. She is Martha, the sister of Mary and Lazarus, a woman who had no trouble telling Jesus her opinions about the way things should be. Martha and her siblings lived together in a house in the town of Bethany during the days of Jesus' earthly ministry. Martha may have been the wife or widow of Simon the Leper, who had also become a follower of Jesus, but the Bible does not tell us if that was the case. We do know from the Gospels that Martha was a woman given to hospitality. It is clear that she had a gift for serving the domestic needs of others, a gift she used to bless Jesus. When Jesus came to Bethany, it was Martha who welcomed him into their home and invited him to dinner. Jesus and the three siblings became intimate friends.

In spite of being sisters, Mary and Martha were very different. Where Mary was quiet and retiring, Martha was vigorously energetic. Mary preferred a passive lifestyle, whereas Martha's was full of activity. The first glimpse we get into Martha's critical spirit unfolds while Jesus was resting at their home. Having invited him to dinner, Martha set about putting together an elaborate meal for Jesus. While she prepared the meal, Jesus sat and talked with Mary. He most surely found the household environment refreshing after steady travel on hot, dusty roads with crowds of people thronging around him unceasingly. The smell of dinner cooking, the careful touches of domesticity throughout the home, and the peace and quiet would have pleased his senses and relaxed his weary body.

Martha was growing increasingly irritated as the hour wore on. She wanted the meal to be just right for Jesus, so the preparations were likely quite elaborate. And there was her sister, Mary, caught up in dreams and thoughts as usual, doing nothing to help. She sat there at Jesus' feet listening to him while she, Martha, did all the work. She was missing out on the conversation. It wasn't fair! Finally her irritation reached its peak, and she turned to Jesus in exasperation and said, "Lord, do You not care that my sister has left me to serve alone? Therefore tell her to help me" (Luke 10:40).

Martha had no qualms about expressing her irritation to Jesus or about asking him to do something to help her. She was straightforward with him in her assessment of the situation, freely pouring forth her complaint. There was work to be done, and she was doing it all. Mary was doing nothing to help. Black and white in her judgment of Mary, Martha criticized her sister for leaving her to serve alone. Notice, too, her criticism of Jesus in the accusation, "Do you not care . . ."

Jesus looked up from his conversation with Mary to answer Martha. He did not say, "How dare you accuse me of not caring!" Nor did he say, "Go away and come back after you have changed your attitude." Rather, he said, "Martha, Martha, you are worried and troubled about many things. But one thing is needed, and Mary has chosen that good part, which will not be taken away from her" (Luke 10:41–42). Jesus is so gentle in his dealings with us, even when we do not offer him the same in turn. Rather than rebuke Martha, he helped her to realize that she was suffering from a sinful case of anxiety. He then came to Mary's defense, and in so doing, he sought to pass along the root of Mary's peace to Martha.

Additionally, Jesus was not saying that Martha's meal preparation was unimportant. He was not implying that work should be cast aside for more spiritual matters. Rather, he was advocating a balance. A less elaborate meal would allow for less preparation, in which case Martha would be free to listen to him along with Mary. Jesus sought to correct Martha's black-and-white evaluation of the situation and impart a little gray into her picture of things.

Jesus gave Martha a gentle but clear answer, and he does the same with us when we are forthright in our prayers. Here, however, Martha not only presented him with the facts as they appeared to her, but she carried her assessment a bit too far. She had her mind made up about the way things were and how they should be. But rather than shun her or disregard her request, he helped her see things in a different light. That is what he does with us, too. As we pour out our hearts and our thoughts to him about everything, he will help us see where we are off base.

Underlying Issues

Martha was painfully honest with Jesus about her feelings. She did not hold back, simmering in a state of anger and frustration. She could easily have thought, "I will not tell him how I feel. It sounds petty, and he will probably get mad at me for making an issue of it." Rather, she pursued honest communication, without compromising her acknowledgement of his lordship. Do you do that, or do you keep your frustrations to yourself, afraid that God might get disgusted with you or annoyed about your attitude? If you are afraid, recalling Martha's relationship with Jesus can help you leave your fear behind. Look what she gained from her honesty with him. Jesus opened her eyes to see what was bothering her—anxiety about something trivial. If we go to him with our complaints, pouring out similar frustrations, God will do no less for us. He will open our eyes to see what is bothering us; he will point out the underlying source of our problem.

Often a critical spirit is a mask for something else. We tend to feel annoyed with others who exhibit the flaws we are secretly aware of in ourselves. Other times our criticism is misplaced. When we are unhappy in our jobs, we find that our co-workers get on our nerves.

The lack of social opportunities in our church can lead us to criticize the preaching and leadership of our pastors. What God will do, if we are honest with him about our irritation, is get at the underlying reason for it, and he will help us to understand why we feel so critical toward someone else or toward him.

Like Martha, do you ever accuse God of not caring about you? When things do not go well, when your hopes are disappointed, or when someone else benefits at your expense, do you feel that God doesn't care? If so, do what Martha did. Tell God how you feel. Keeping those thoughts and feelings locked up inside yourself will only cause you to feel distant from the source of help and love most available to you. God invites your honesty. He desires to communicate with his people. The greatest of saints have accepted God's invitation in difficult circumstances. One of the psalmists cried, "Lord, why do You cast off my soul? Why do You hide Your face from me? I have been afflicted and ready to die from my youth; I suffer your terrors; I am distraught" (Ps. 88:14–15). Job is another example, as is Jeremiah. Just so, Martha was helped out of her critical attitude that day by taking it to Jesus. But her tendency to criticism still lurked within her heart. As of yet, no gray had emerged to soften the remaining hard edges of black and white.

But, Lord . . .

We learn that from a story recounted in the Gospel of John. Lazarus, her brother, was stricken with a serious illness and when his life appeared to be in danger, Martha and Mary sent for Jesus, who was in another town carrying out his ministry. "When Jesus heard that, He said, 'This sickness is not unto death, but for the glory of God, that the Son of God may be glorified through it.' Now Jesus loved Martha and her sister and Lazarus. So when He heard that he was sick, He stayed two more days in the place where He was" (John 11:4–6). We are not told whether or not Jesus' response was delivered to Martha and Mary. But by the time Jesus reached Bethany, Lazarus had been dead for four days.

Martha and Mary were at home, surrounded by friends, grieving over the death of their beloved brother. Word came to the house that Jesus was close by, only about two miles away. So Martha ran out to meet him. He was on his way to their house when she found him. She said, "Lord, if You had been here, my brother would not have died. But even now I know that whatever You ask of God, God will give you" (John 11:21–22). Just as before, Martha ran to Jesus with her trouble. Yet once again the first words out of her mouth were filled with criticism.

Their conversation continued. "Jesus said to her, 'Your brother will rise again.' Martha said to Him, 'I know that he will rise again in the resurrection at the last day' " (John 11:23–24). Martha was adopting a stiff upper lip, trying to find acceptance in the pain of her loss. But Jesus still had not answered her accusation. Why had he not arrived sooner and so saved her brother's life? He obviously knew her thoughts, because he continued to draw her out. "Jesus said to her, 'I am the resurrection and the life. He who believes in Me, though he may die, he shall live. And whoever lives and believes in Me shall never die. Do you believe this?' " (John 11:25–26). Jesus was not being evasive. He was in the process of rooting out Martha's critical spirit, and he did that by refocusing her thoughts onto him, his power, his care, and his glory. It worked, because Martha answered him, "Yes, Lord, I believe that You are the Christ, the Son of God, who is to come into the world" (John 11:27).

God comes to us in the same way. When we are perplexed by his ways, when he allows something tragic that we do not understand, he usually will not tell us why. Instead he will reveal himself to our hurting hearts. God has never promised to give us explanations for what he does. What he has promised is hope, help, and healing in the midst of it. That is what he held out to Martha when she came to him in her grief. So with Jesus by her side she went back to the house where Mary and the others were grieving.

Mary came out to him and fell at his feet, echoing Martha's accusation. "Lord, if You had been here, my brother would not have died" (John 11:32). We read that when Jesus saw the mourners and the great grief of the two sisters, he was troubled in his spirit and began to weep. The Lord is not like we are. If someone comes accusing us of misconduct, we are not likely to be overtaken with compassion for our accuser. But that is what God does. He knows our hurts, and even when we blame him for our pain, he does not cease to comfort and heal.

The best part was still to come. Jesus and the mourners ambled to the tomb where Lazarus had been buried, and when the group arrived there, Jesus asked someone to roll away the stone covering the entrance. Practical Martha intervened at that point, saying, "Lord, by this time there is a stench, for he has been dead four days" (John 11:39). It was then that Jesus blessed her beyond anything she had imagined. He said to her, "Did I not say to you that if you would believe you would see the glory of God?" (John 11:40). After Jesus offered up prayer to God and the stone had been rolled away, he commanded, " 'Lazarus, come forth!' And he who had died came out bound hand and foot with graveclothes and his face was wrapped with a cloth. Jesus said to them, 'Loose him, and let him go' " (John 11:43–44). Martha never got her explanation, but she got something better. Once again she had been quick to criticize, size up the situation, pass judgment on what had happened, and articulate what she thought should have been done instead. And once again, Jesus ministered to Martha in the gentle way she needed.

Up Close and Personal

Martha learned several things about Jesus that day, things that will benefit you if you are perplexed about something. Are you angry with God? Do you feel that he has acted unfairly or turned his face away when you need him most? If you find that you are accusing him in your heart, he wants you to bring your hurts to him. Tell him exactly what you are thinking and feeling. When you do, you will find what

Martha found, namely, that God's patience is infinite. He will not turn away from you. Rather, he will welcome you into his presence. God delights in honesty. He also is a realist. He knows everything we think and why we think it. Far from being sinful, telling God of your complaint, your anger, and your frustration is an act of humility, so long as you approach him with the reverence he is due. By approaching God with complete honesty mingled with respect and awe, you are inviting him to respond to you.

If you will do that, you will learn what Martha learned about how God responds. Rather than stooping down to your level, he will lift you up to his. He will redirect your thoughts according to the truth of his Word, and when that happens, you will begin to see things in a new light. God does not do this to avoid your accusations or to lull you into complacency in the midst of difficulty. Rather, he does it because when you see things in the light of his Word, you see things as they are, which, for his children, always means peace and healing. Are you a black-and-white woman like Martha, prone to pass judgment in a spirit of criticism before knowing all the facts? If so, you will avoid a lot of frustration, mental anguish, and isolation if you pour yourself into God's Word. Scripture will help you the same way that Jesus helped Martha. The voice she heard and the words we read are one and the same.

Martha also learned that her critical attitude toward Jesus was misplaced, because he was worthy of her unqualified trust. She discovered that delays do not necessarily mean no. Have you been crying out to God in your pain and finding him silent about your need? Rest assured that he has not abandoned you to your suffering. He is not waiting for you to get yourself together and get on with life. He does have an answer, a specific solution, to what is causing you distress or agony. In his perfect time he will reveal it to you. So wait for it, because his perfect time will be the point at which he is most glorified and the one at which you will praise him most and love him more as a result.

20

The Samaritan Woman
Satisfaction Guaranteed

Chosen and Cherished

The earthly life of Jesus Christ was relatively short, a mere thirty-three years, but in that brief span of time, countless aspects of his nature were revealed and recorded for us in the Gospels. We learn what makes him angry and what causes him grief. We witness the way he deals with people, whether in the intimacy of friendship or through his patience among the crowds. Another thing we see is the great compassion that Jesus has for women, especially for those who are poor, lonely, or unliked by other people.

Evidence of such compassion is seen throughout his life and ministry. Jesus treated his mother, Mary, with the utmost respect and provided for her future in the midst of his greatest agony on the cross. He delivered Mary Magdalene from seven demons. He healed a woman who had been hemorrhaging for twelve years, a woman whose illness had rendered her unclean, a social outcast. He publicly pardoned a woman caught in adultery, a sin for which the customary penalty was death. Assuredly his heart for these women contributed to the criticism leveled against him by a suspicious public. In an age where women

were second-class citizens, Jesus' care for them astounded some and
angered others. Jesus crossed many cultural barriers to reach women.

Jesus and the Sin-Sick Soul

Nowhere is this more evident than in an incident when Jesus met a
woman one day on his way to Galilee from Judea. Customarily, devout
Jews traveled in a roundabout way when making that journey in order
to avoid Samaria. Contempt between Jews and Samaritans had developed over centuries, and racial tensions ran high. But Jesus held no
prejudices and he undertook his trip by going straight through the
despised region. At about noontime, Jesus came to Jacob's well, and he
stopped there to rest. He had sent the disciples into town to buy food
so he was by himself when, a few minutes later, a local woman came
along to draw water. She was evidently poor because affluent women
did not perform such tasks in Jesus' day. He asked the woman for a drink
of the water she was drawing, so she asked him, "How is it that You,
being a Jew, ask a drink from me, a Samaritan woman?" (John 4:9).

Jesus responded, "If you knew the gift of God, and who it is who
says to you, 'Give me a drink,' you would have asked Him, and He
would have given you living water" (John 4:10). Jesus was holding
out to this woman the gift of himself, but she did not yet understand
that. She was not thinking in spiritual terms. She thought Jesus was
telling her about another well from which she could obtain her water
supply. Jesus went on to say, "Whoever drinks of this water will thirst
again, but whoever drinks of the water that I shall give him will never
thirst. But the water that I shall give him will become in him a foun-
tain of water springing up into everlasting life" (John 4:13–14). Jesus'
words appealed to her earthly mindset, so she said, "Sir, give me this
water, that I may not thirst, nor come here to draw" (John 4:15).

What Jesus said next got the woman thinking along different lines.
He said, "Go, call your husband, and come here" (John 4:16). She
must have paused to think about her answer. In her case it was a difficult thing to discuss. But when she answered, she did so honestly.

She said, "I have no husband" (John 4:17a). Jesus already knew that, of course. He was merely doing what he always does when he brings us to salvation, and that is to make us aware of our sin. He continued, "You have well said, 'I have no husband,' for you have had five husbands, and the one whom you now have is not your husband; in that you spoke truly" (John 4:18). Although speaking gently, Jesus is confronting the woman with her immorality. It is only through facing up to what we have been and all we have done to violate God's laws that we become aware of our need for the living water that only Jesus can supply.

Jesus went on to tell her what he admitted to few people at that time: that he was the long-promised Messiah. As the truth began to dawn in her heart, the disciples returned and were surprised to find Jesus speaking with a woman. At that point she left her water jugs and ran into the city to tell others about this strange man. She told them all, "Come, see a Man who told me all things that I ever did. Could this be the Christ?" (John 4:29). And when they had heard her words, they came to the well to see about this man. It is interesting to note that it was she who brought the Samaritans to see Jesus, and not the disciples, who had just come from the city. Her excitement was contagious and effective.

Although not fully realizing the import of what had happened to her that day, she knew that this Jewish man with an aura of authority had reached out to offer her something valuable, even though he knew what she was and all that she had done. Since we have the whole story of Jesus, we can see what she could not see, namely, that Jesus yearned to give this woman what she lacked. It was no accident that he met her at the well. He came there and sent his disciples away in preparation for her arrival at that spot, so when she came upon him, he was waiting for her. That is always the case. Jesus is waiting for us to come while simultaneously he is drawing us to him so that he can give us himself.

Have you found him? He is waiting for you, too, no matter what your life is like now or what dark secrets lie in your past. The Samaritan woman was surprised that he reached out to her because she knew she was despised. The Jews shunned her for her nationality, and most likely, many of her own people scorned her for living with a man not her husband. Yet suddenly here was someone who knew everything about her, condescending to speak with her and offer her a precious gift besides. And Jesus ached for this woman. In his commentary on John's Gospel, Pastor James Montgomery Boice wrote, "What a picture of Jesus! Here was a Jesus who was not wearied merely by the heat. He could have stayed in the cooler area of the Jordan. Here was a Jesus who was wearied in his search for sinners and who would become thirsty seeking those to whom he was to offer the water of life. On the same errand he would experience an even greater thirst on the cross."[1]

Dr. Boice went on to quote missionary Geoffrey Bull, who wrote, "If she could have seen just then what Jesus saw, she would have glimpsed another noonday when the sun would mourn in blackness and this same Stranger cry out from a Roman cross, 'I thirst!' She would have seen in him the shadow of a great rock in a weary land, the smitten Christ from whom the living waters flow. . . . He was thirstier than she knew. He was speaking for the very heart of God. He was moving in the travail of his soul and looked for satisfaction in the restoration of this sin-scarred woman."[2]

A Deeper Well and a Better Way

Jesus knew what this woman needed, and he got to the heart of the matter. "Go, call your husband," he said. Not only was she living with the contempt of others; she held within her the shame that immoral behavior always brings. Jesus came to offer her love in place of the contempt and freedom from her shame. Yet she needed something else also. "I have no husband," she answered Jesus. It is obvious from the number of men with which she had lived that she had become used to seeking provision and solace by linking herself to men, one after another. But again and again that had failed to provide her with what she really yearned for.

All five husbands had died, we assume, and this sixth man, for whatever reason, had not married her. She had not been able to find that for which she so deeply yearned. Yet she could not fathom another way to cope with life, so she bore the shame. She needed someone who would never leave her and who would treat her with respect and dignity. What she most needed was a true Savior. Jesus brought her to himself and offered her all of that.

A great many women today view their relationships with men in the same deceitful light as did the Samaritan woman. At some level they do not believe that they are complete or safe without a man. They need the illumination of Christ, just as she did. They are thinking like the Samaritan woman, who, in her initial conversation with Jesus, couldn't grasp spiritual truths. "Sir, give me this water, that I may not thirst, nor come here to draw," she had said. She could comprehend only earthly realities.

There are, however, an equal number of women who already know Christ, yet they suffer from the same problem. They profess Christ as Lord and Savior, but they devote much of themselves to finding something or someone else with which to connect. They have already received the living water Christ holds out, yet they are not drinking it. Instead they are standing by the well on a hot and dusty day looking for another water supply. Perhaps you are one of these women. You can test yourself by honestly asking if you have found Jesus to be the satisfier of your soul, or whether it is always Jesus plus something else that you think you need.

Those of you who have not found Jesus to be sufficient for all your needs might merely need a deeper understanding of the living water Jesus holds out to us. Water, in and of itself, is something we take for granted in Western society. We have it in abundance whenever we need it. It is accessible in six-packs and big gallon jugs. Water coolers reside on every floor in many office buildings. We can draw it up hot or cold at whim. We complain if the water pressure in the shower fails to produce a pounding spray, and on those rare occasions when droughts hit and water restrictions go into effect, we complain about unwashed cars and wilting gardens.

But that was not the case in Jesus' day. Water was not easily come by. The Samaritan woman had to walk some distance to draw water for simple household use. And for all that effort, the need for more water was perpetual. Jesus' comparison of salvation with living water would have had great impact on the Samaritan woman. So to put it in a context we can understand, think of thirst as anything for which you long but which you cannot seem to obtain. Whatever that is, Jesus is the living answer to that need. Is your thirst loneliness? Jesus can fulfill your longing in a permanent way. Perhaps you thirst for love, or for meaning and purpose. Jesus longs to provide you with all of that. Living water represents complete satisfaction.

Jesus was holding out freedom to the Samaritan woman. She was free to leave her life of immorality. Jesus could provide her with everything she had sought from her husbands and her live-in boyfriend. That is true of us as well. When Jesus saves us, he is setting us free not to sin. Before we are saved, we are not free not to sin. We know nothing else. But when the Holy Spirit illuminates our hearts and offers us the true and eternal living water, our hearts are opened to a new way of life. That is why neediness is never a reason or an excuse to sin. If we lack something on the earthly plane, it is only so God can give us something better. And in reality, if we have him, we lack nothing.

Delight for the Downcast

Do you want to know Jesus' living water for yourself? Certainly you do! Do not let shame about your life hold you back. If Jesus is confronting you with your sin, it is to show you how much you need him. He wants you to do what the Samaritan woman did. Be honest with him about it. He already knows it fully anyway. So be honest with him and with yourself. It is on that basis that you will know your thirst, the need you have for the water that cleanses you from all that sin.

Whatever long, hot road you are traveling, whatever cares are weighing you down, if you are lonely, outcast, and scorned by others, Jesus has a special heart for you. He is waiting to take care of all that. He longs to give you himself in place of your sin and your troubles. He is waiting by the well for you.

21

Sapphira

A Fate Worse Than Death

True Happiness

What is the first thing that comes to mind when you think about holiness? For some of us the idea of holiness conjures up images of cathedral sanctuaries, hushed in their massive grandeur. Others think more in terms of stringent living, adhering to a strict observance of all God's laws. The word *holiness* does not ring joyful in the ears of many; instead it carries somber connotations. To those who think that way, God's command to be holy is about as appealing as embarking on a diet or a tight budget. But holiness is not like that. Far from delivering us into the bondage of restriction, it frees us. That is because to be holy means to be set apart for God, for fellowship with him, and for work in his service. The process by which we become holy is called sanctification, and it occurs as we become conformed to the image of Jesus Christ.

Holiness does entail obeying God's commandments, but there is so much more to it than a set of rules. For one thing, as we grow in holiness the fruits of the Spirit are produced in our lives. Those fruits include such things as love, joy, peace, patience, kindness, goodness, faithfulness, gentleness, and self-control (Gal. 5:22–23). Holiness includes all of the blessings, spiritual and material, that are part of our inheritance through Jesus Christ. Holiness is also linked inextricably to true beauty. Psalm 96:9 proclaims, "Oh, worship the LORD in the beauty of holiness!" Far from being a drudgery, it always goes hand in hand with joy, because God has ordained that our happiness is bound up in holiness.

Our personal holiness also matters intensely to God because it is a reflection of his character. God is pure, undiluted holiness. Holiness is a synonym for perfection. When the glory of God's holiness reflects off of us, even the shadow of it, he is glorified before all who witness it. The writer of Hebrews stated, "Pursue peace with all people, and holiness, without which no one will see the Lord" (Heb. 12:14). Others around us see God through whatever measure of holiness we exude.

Because God knows that holiness leads to his glory and our happiness, it is of crucial importance to him. In fact, he will go to great lengths to produce holiness in his people and to preserve them in it. We find the great emphasis God places on holiness throughout the Bible. From the days of Moses, God said, "You shall be holy; for I am holy" (Lev. 11:44). The apostle Peter quoted those words when he wrote, "As He who called you is holy, you also be holy in all your conduct, because it is written, 'Be holy, for I am holy'" (1 Peter 1:15–16). God has called us to a lifestyle of holiness.

Every believer is destined for holiness. As Paul wrote to the Ephesians: "Blessed be the God and Father of our Lord Jesus Christ, who has blessed us with every spiritual blessing in the heavenly places in Christ, just as He chose us in Him before the foundation of the world, that we should be holy and without blame before Him in love" (Eph. 1:3–4).

A Fate Worse Than Death

Understanding the emphasis God places on holiness helps us understand the tragic story of Sapphira and her husband, Ananias, a short account in the book of Acts. Ananias and Sapphira were an integral part of the small but growing Christian community that flourished in the days after Christ's death and resurrection. The early church lived communally, that is, they pooled their resources for the daily benefit and welfare of the group. Luke, the author of Acts, tells us, "Now the multitude of those who believed were of one heart and one soul; neither did anyone say that any of the things he possessed was his own, but they had all things in common" (Acts 4:32). Further, "Nor was there anyone among them who lacked; for all who were possessors of lands or houses sold them, and brought the proceeds of the things that were sold, and laid them at the apostles' feet; and they distributed to each as anyone had need" (Acts 4:34–35).

Ananias and Sapphira were among those who owned land, and, as part of the Christian community, they determined to sell it as the other believers were doing with their possessions. After doing so, however, they talked together and decided to keep some of the profit for themselves rather than turning everything over to the group. The couple set aside some of the money; then Ananias took the remainder of the proceeds to the apostles to be used for the common good. But rather than being straightforward about their decision to keep some of the money for themselves, Ananias lied to the group.

The apostle Peter had been granted the special gift of discernment, so he knew that Ananias was not being truthful. He said, "Ananias, why has Satan filled your heart to lie to the Holy Spirit and keep back part of the price of the land for yourself? While it remained, was it not your own? And after it was sold, was it not in your own control? Why have you conceived this thing in your heart? You have not lied to men but to God" (Acts 5:3–4).

From Peter's words, it is obvious that Ananias's sin was not about withholding some of his profit; rather, it was about the lie he told. As Peter pointed out, the land belonged to Ananias and Sapphira; they were free to do with it as they wished. If they wanted to keep some of the money for themselves, they had the freedom to do so. God desires our giving to be cheerful and generous, not compulsory. In fact, it is better not to give than to give for the approval of man or out of fear. The approval of man obviously had motivated Ananias and Sapphira. They had witnessed the generosity of others in the community, and very likely, they were worried what others would think if they did not share their possessions in like fashion. The fact that they withheld some of the profit indicates that they were not cheerful givers, that what they were seeking was the high regard of the apostles and the other believers. Therefore, their greater sins were hypocrisy, vanity, and, worst of all, as Peter pointed out, lying to the Holy Spirit.

Immediately after Peter exposed Ananias's falsehood, a horrifying thing happened, something that shocked and terrified all those watching: Ananias fell down to the ground and died instantly. In awe and fright, those who were present wrapped up his body, took him out, and buried him. A few hours later, Sapphira came in looking for her husband. She had no idea what had happened. She must have sensed something was wrong, however, when Peter questioned her about the sale of the land. He wanted to see whether Sapphira was involved in the deception, so he asked her how much money she and her husband had received in the sale. Sapphira stuck to the story she and Ananias had agreed to tell, and she echoed her husband's lie to Peter.

Then, as he had said to Ananias three hours earlier, Peter said to Sapphira, "How is it that you have agreed together to test the Spirit of the Lord? Look, the feet of those who have buried your husband are at the door, and they will carry you out" (Acts 5:9). Immediately Sapphira fell down dead and was taken out and buried beside her husband.

The small Christian community was stunned. "Great fear came upon all the church and upon all who heard these things" (Acts 5:11). It is easy to understand why the event brought fear to those who witnessed the deaths. It was not as though Ananias and Sapphira had committed murder or some other capital offense. A mere lie, a bit of hypocrisy, and they were struck dead by God! Everyone within the community knew in their hearts that they were each capable of the same sins. Would they be next? Would God strike them down? Why would God, the One whom they had come to know as Father, act in such a way?

A Life-or-Death Matter

The death of an individual is one of the secret things of God. "The secret things belong to the LORD our God, but those things which are revealed belong to us and to our children forever that we may do all the words of this law" (Deut. 29:29). This means that although God teaches us certain truths through death and other matters, we cannot ever assume we know God's purposes in them. All that we are given to know for sure is found only in the Bible. So from the teaching of Scripture overall, what can we infer from the deaths of Ananias and Sapphira? From their story, it is safe to infer that God will go to great lengths to preserve his holiness. Through this shocking event an important truth was established in those early days of the church. God was ensuring that this small but growing body of believers would be established on the firm foundation of God's true character, his holy character.

Additionally, in the days following the death and resurrection of Jesus, people outside the church were closely observing the Christians. They were watching to see what would become of them now that their leader was no longer in their midst. Would all this talk of the coming of God's kingdom fade away? Had the Messiah really even come? Evidence would come through the conduct of his remaining followers.

In the deaths of Sapphira and her husband, God was making a point to those within the church and to those on the outside who were watching. In a startling way, God conveyed that although salvation is not by works but only through grace and faith, the requirement for holiness in his people had not changed one iota.

Yet understanding that still leaves us with some unanswered questions. First, how can a God of love kill one of his own? And does God still put people to death for their sins? If so, how can we know that it will not happen to us? Finally, is there anything we can learn from Sapphira to apply to our lives?

What we learn from Sapphira has less to do with her than it does with what her story shows us about God. From her we see God's strong determination to save us, even at the expense of our earthly lives. God has foreordained all those who are to inherit eternal life, and not one of them shall be lost. Romans 8 teaches us that "all things work together for good to those who love God, to those who are the called according to His purpose. For whom He foreknew, He also predestined to be conformed to the image of His Son, that He might be the firstborn among many brethren. Moreover whom He predestined, these He also called; whom He called, these He also justified; and whom He justified, these He also glorified" (Rom. 8:28–30). That means that there is no way we can lose our salvation. God will never let us go. If we have been brought into the kingdom of God through the sacrifice of Jesus Christ, you and I can never sin so badly that we will reverse or eradicate our inheritance.

We can also better understand Sapphira's untimely death if we have the right perspective of life on this earth. Eternal life is much more valuable than our earthly existence. Life here is like the blink of an eye compared with our later life in heaven. Not only was God zealous to protect his holiness before those who were watching; he also was ensuring Sapphira's eternal status. One of the reasons we cannot lose salvation by our sin is that God will occasionally end an earthly life to prevent such loss. James Montgomery Boice occasionally pointed out in his sermons that we need not fear the loss of God's eternal favor by falling into a backslidden condition, because, he said, if you backslide to that degree, God will do one of two things. Either he will make you so miserable that you will beg him to get you out of it, or he will take your life away.

If that were the case with Sapphira, God took away her earthly life in order to preserve her for all eternity. Paul's words to the Romans expressly show that neither death nor life can destroy a true believer. He wrote, "For I am persuaded that neither death nor life, nor angels nor principalities nor powers, nor things present nor things to come, nor height nor depth, nor any other created thing, shall able to separate us from the love of God which is in Christ Jesus our Lord" (Rom. 8:38–39). Neither life nor death, nor any other created thing, including our sin, can make him stop loving us. The fact that God killed Sapphira does not mean that God ceased to love her. On the contrary, if she were truly saved, it was a sign of his favor.

This leads us to wonder whether a lie and a bit of hypocrisy are the sort of sins that would place our earthly lives in jeopardy, and if, like Sapphira, our lives are, therefore, also in danger since we are guilty of such sins daily. But we need not worry because what concerns God is whether our hearts are moving steadily, however slowly, toward him rather than falling away. So we need not walk around in a constant state of fear; it is much more beneficial to realize that God evaluates our hearts and actions very differently from how we judge them, and he alone knows what it will take to preserve each of us individually. What was necessary for Sapphira may be different from what is necessary to preserve you and me. Remember also that God was setting an example through Sapphira and her husband for the young church and generations to follow, making clear that holiness matters just as much in the new age where we are governed by grace as it did in the former age that was governed by law.

The story of Sapphira, therefore, is meant to serve as a warning to all believers, as well as a sign of hope. The warning is important to ponder as you consider your growth in holiness. Is personal holiness a priority for you? One way to measure that for yourself is by the intensity of your desire for God. If you delight to spend time with him in worship, in prayer, and reading his Word, then you are growing in holiness. If you long to know those things that please him so that you can practice them, you are pursuing holiness. If you find yourself obeying even a fraction more fully than in days gone by, you are exhibiting greater holiness. On the other hand, if the things of God matter little to you, if you are trifling with something you know is displeasing to God, than you stand in danger of God's discipline. Just as with Sapphira, God will do whatever it takes to preserve us for him, even when that discipline is painful and costly.

If you are not sure you understand what it means to be holy, why not read all that the Bible has to say about it? Using a concordance, look up in the Old and New Testaments several references that contain the word *holy* or *holiness*. If you would like to do some further reading on the topic, I suggest J. C. Ryle's *Holiness*. Another good book is *The Pursuit of Holiness* by Jerry Bridges.

Love That Won't Let Go

Some years ago, I read a magazine article about a Christian counselor who fell into an age-old sin. In spite of being married for several decades to a delightful woman whom he loved dearly, he became charmed by Martina, an attractive younger woman who had sought his counsel for her troubled marriage. Contained in the magazine article was a short interview with Martina. The interview revealed that the Christian counselor and Martina had begun over time to extend their relationship beyond the boundaries of its professional context. They spent a lot of one-on-one time together, building a level of intimacy inappropriate and dangerous for two people who were both married to other people. Inevitably, they fell in love. A short time later the counselor was killed in an auto accident.

Many people grieved his death, perhaps none with more pain than Martina. That was because she was weighed down with guilt. I was struck by something she said in the magazine interview: "I can't help but think that I killed him! Maybe God took his life away before our relationship could destroy his ministry." What struck me about her remarks is the possibility that her fear may be well founded. Although we may never assume that we know the reasons for what God does, the possibility exists that he may well have ended the counselor's earthly life to preserve many from the destruction that such a relationship inevitably brings. If allowed to continue, the immoral relationship could easily have destroyed the counselor's fruitful ministry.

God loves you and me enough to do the same with our lives if necessary. So back to the question about personal holiness. Does it matter to you? It matters intensely to God. And remember, those who grow in holiness also grow in happiness. Pursue it with all your heart, and you will find untold freedom and a whole new way to enjoy your life.

22

Lydia

Green Grass in Your Back Yard

Greener Grass

Jenny breezed into the party on Clayton's arm, a frozen smile on her face. She was petrified with anxiety about tonight, the biggest event of the year for all the associates in Clayton's law firm. Masquerading as a social occasion, the evening was the final deciding factor as to which of the associates would be made partners in the firm. It all hinged on how witty they would be at dinner, how they charmed the partners' wives, and the evidence of social graces exhibited by their own wives. Jenny knew how important tonight was, and the important role she played in determining Clayton's future.

As she surveyed the room her heart dropped. "This pink dress is all wrong!" she thought. "Everyone else is wearing black! One strike against us already." Jenny sat down for dinner feeling miserable and tongue-tied. The other women at her table were carrying on about an upcoming socialite fundraiser, a conversation to which Jenny had nothing to contribute. What with teaching three weekly Bible studies, cooking each day for the homeless ministry at church, and making a nice home for Clayton, Jenny had little time left for other activities.

Shortly before the meal was served, Jenny excused herself and escaped to the ladies' room. Once there, however, several other women came in together and stood near Jenny as she pretended to fix her make-up. Jenny couldn't help but overhear their conversation, and she cringed at the sarcastic remarks, most of them veiling resentment and dissatisfaction with their husbands. "Grant better be made partner," one woman threatened. "I'm sick of living on his current salary."

"I know what you mean," another answered. "I'll die of embarrassment if Jack doesn't make it. I'll simply go into seclusion!"

"Not to mention five years of twelve-hour work days," a third chimed in. "All that time at the office. Always at the beck and call of the firm. Like eager puppy dogs panting for crumbs!" Female laughter rippled and echoed off the mirror.

"What about you?" one of them asked Jenny. "Aren't you Clayton's wife? You're in the same boat as the rest of us. Aren't you sick of living like this?" As they waited for her response, indignation loosened Jenny's tongue. She thought of Clayton's hard work, the hours and days of sacrifice he'd poured out in order to be a witness for Christ to his co-workers and to provide a comfortable if modest life for her. "I'm not sick of it at all!" she responded. "I'm glad that he loves his work. I'm also glad that I have a husband with a strong work ethic."

The silence was tangible for a moment or two, then, "But, Jenny, does that mean you don't care whether or not Clayton makes partner?" "Of course I care," Jenny replied, "but I care for his sake. He's worked so hard. He has earned it. I want to see my husband's dedication rewarded."

Jenny went back to her table with no regrets. Even if her comments had caused her and Clayton social damage, supporting and encouraging her husband was the important thing.

Later, after dinner, Jenny escaped again to the ladies' room in hope of a few moments of quiet. While she reapplied her lipstick, another wife appeared beside her. "You're Jenny, right?" she asked.

"I'm Michelle. I was right outside the door earlier when you spoke up to those women! I couldn't help but notice how different you are from the rest of them. The way you stuck up for your husband. I don't think I would have had the courage to say what you did! It made me ashamed of myself. In fact, you helped me see our husbands' work in a whole new light. They really are hard workers, and they do it for us."

At the end of the evening, all the associates and their wives passed through a receiving line where they were greeted by the partners and their wives. As Jenny and Clayton neared the door, she was introduced to an elderly man, the senior partner, and as he shook her hand, he said to Clayton, "This is quite a wife you have here." He chuckled and said, "The words of women travel fast. I've already heard about a certain conversation held in the ladies' room this evening. Supportive wives make for happy husbands, and men like that are able to give their best to the firm. You're just the sort of man we want for partner, Clayton." They drove home in a state of euphoria. "I was so worried that my lack of sophistication would hurt your career," Jenny confessed. "God is so good!"

Jenny is beginning to learn an important truth: when we focus on and envy the talents of others, we fail to see our unique gifts. Jenny has often felt insecure due to her lack of worldly sophistication. From girlhood, she has admired women who have a knack for fitting in socially, the sort of woman who never fails to show up with the right outfit, one who carries on witty and interesting conversations with crowds of people. Jenny is so focused on the gifts other women possess that she fails to see how her gift of encouragement, her sensitivity, and her gentle demeanor serve to comfort and strengthen those around her.

Getting Started

Perhaps you are like Jenny. You see women all around you, believers and unbelievers, who exude confidence. They breeze from one activity to the next, meeting their goals and making the most of every opportunity. You wonder why things seem so easy for them. What is their secret? It is no great mystery. These women merely know and understand what they are good at. They have discovered their gifts and put them to use.

For Christian women, there are two additional considerations necessary for successful living. The first consideration is for what or whom are you working; in other words, what is your motivation? Anything short of God's glory is an unworthy motive and will not produce anything of eternal value. The second consideration is submission. You will find yourself accomplishing much once you have accepted the things God has equipped you to do, rather than longing for the gifts God has given to someone else. We will always be good at what we are called to do.

If you are a Christian, God has provided you with natural talents and spiritual gifts. There are differences between talents and gifts. Your talents have been with you from birth. They are part of what is called God's common grace, meaning that they are a blessing reserved not only for Christians but one that is bestowed on mankind at large. God's common grace is a term used by theologians to refer to the exercise of God's goodness toward all he has created. We see common grace at work wherever there is goodness, prosperity, or happiness in the world and in the people all around us, regardless of their standing in God's kingdom. In speaking of God the Father, Jesus said, "He makes His sun rise on the evil and on the good, and sends rain on the just and on the unjust" (Matt. 5:45). This is common grace.

Spiritual gifts come only to Christians, and they are given to us for use in the body of Christ. You can find lists of spiritual gifts in the New Testament in Romans 12:6–8, in 1 Corinthians 12:4–11, and in Ephesians 4:7–12. We can use our talents in all kinds of ways, for ourselves and for God. Spiritual gifts are not meant for our use but rather for building up the family of Christ into spiritual maturity. When God issues a calling to us, he may and often does incorporate our natural talents into it, but his calling will always involve, in large measure, our spiritual gift or gifts.

A Life Well Lived

Lydia is an example of a woman who made full use of both her natural talents and her spiritual gifts. Living in the Macedonian city of Philippi, Lydia was a businesswoman from the city of Thyatira, a region famous for its superior cloth dye called purple. This purple dye was not exactly like the color we know by that name. Its hues were of a much larger range. That ancient dye produced fabric shades ranging from reddish crimson to various shades of blue. The dye was expensive and, therefore, usually unavailable to those of modest means. From Lydia's story, which appears in Acts 16, we can assume that she was unmarried. There is no mention of a husband; that, and the fact that she supported herself leads us to that inference. The story informs us that Lydia provided a home for others as well. We are not told whether these were relatives or servants. If she was a widow, they may have been her children or other relatives.

Lydia was evidently a woman of independent spirit, unafraid of crowds, rough merchants, and the necessity of conducting her business in a male-dominated environment. She was apparently quite successful in her business enterprises, enough so that she was able to maintain a household for herself and others. Although she was not yet a Christian, her heart yearned after the things of God, so when Lydia was not working, she would gather with local Jewish women at the riverside to read and talk about the Scriptures. That is what Lydia was doing one day when the apostle Paul came down to the river to pray. When no synagogue was nearby, Jews would gather for prayer outdoors near water. Paul had come to Philippi for the very reason of sharing the gospel, so when he came upon the group of women studying God's law, he sat down to talk to them.

Luke was with Paul at this time. Later, when he wrote the book of Acts, Luke recounted what happened to Lydia as Paul shared the gospel: "The Lord opened her heart to heed the thing spoken by Paul" (Acts 16:14). That was the moment of Lydia's conversion to faith in Christ. It happened to her just as it happens to us. Through the Holy Spirit, God enabled her to understand and receive salvation through Jesus Christ. And along with Lydia's salvation came spiritual gifts, and in her case, the gift of hospitality came quickly to light. We read that "when she and her household were baptized, she begged us, saying, 'If you have judged me to be faithful to the Lord, come to my house and stay.' So she persuaded us" (Acts 16:15).

Although Lydia may have had a natural aptitude for entertaining, we can infer that her invitation of hospitality issued also from a newly received spiritual gift, one that she exercised immediately on behalf of fellow believers. Her invitation was not about providing social entertainment but rather was issued to provide comfort and support to others as they were doing the Lord's work.

As is true with all spiritual gifts, we are able to perform them well with the help of the Holy Spirit. That was true in Lydia's case. We know that the apostles found the refreshment they were in need of because Lydia's home was the first place to which they turned after a harrowing experience a short time later. Paul and his co-worker Silas angered the local magistrates, and the two apostles were dragged off to prison and beaten severely. Later that same night Paul and Silas were released. "So they went out of the prison and entered the house of Lydia; and when they had seen the brethren, they encouraged them and departed" (Acts 16:40). Paul and Silas gravitated to Lydia's home, because, through the exercise of her gift, she was enabled to provide a haven for them.

We admire Lydia for her natural talents and for her spiritual gifts, but we all can do as much as she did. The reason Lydia was so successful in business was that she pursued and developed those things at which she naturally excelled. Possessing an independent nature, the ability to hold her ground and be shrewd in bargaining and other matters of finance, and the courage to live against the cultural standards of acceptable feminine behavior, Lydia was a natural for success in the dye business.

As far as her spiritual gift of hospitality, she was able to perform that well because God had provided her with everything she needed to carry it out. Either through her business success or by some other means, God had given Lydia a house suitable for the exercise of her gift. When God gifts us to serve the body of Christ, he always provides the means through which those gifts may be maximized.

Overcoming Obstacles

What are you good at, and what are you doing with it? Are you making use of the gifts and talents with which God has equipped you? I know a good number of women who are frustrated about this very thing. Some of them are devoting the majority of their waking hours to pursuits for which they have not been gifted. Often that is merely part of the necessary process of discovering our calling. Our way is frequently made clear to us through trial and error. God is not in a hurry, and we can trust him to lead as he deems best. Other times women are frustrated because they are coveting gifts and talents that are different from those that God has given them. When that happens, if we fall into that way of thinking, we will spend much time and energy trying to become good at something for which we are not well suited. And although it is good to stretch ourselves outside of our comfort zones, devoting our lives to something for which we are not naturally gifted eventually results in frustration.

I have a close friend named Olivia who is gifted as a teacher. Olivia is aware of her superior skills, both from her personal academic success and from what others have told her. After completing four years of college, followed immediately by an intensive graduate program in education, Olivia pursued a career in sales, a field for which none of her education or previous experience had prepared her. Olivia's choice puzzled many who knew her at the time. Although such a career requires education and good deal of smarts, it did not seem the best choice for someone of her particular talents.

Now, several years later, Olivia is unhappy in her career and questioning her former decision. She is seeking to discover how she can best use the talents and gifts God has given her, not only for her fulfillment but also for his glory. In fact, seeking to bring God glory in how we exercise our gifts and talents is of primary importance. It is also true that seeking his honor always goes hand in hand with personal fulfillment for us. I know Olivia will find it, because her quest has become that of honoring God above every other consideration.

Envy of the gifts of others robs God of his glory and steals from us a sense of satisfaction and well-being about our lives. It is truly important to value and make use of your gifts because you have been called to fulfill a unique function in the Christian community where God has placed you. Lydia's gift of hospitality and God's provision for the carrying out of her gift provided for the apostles what others among them were not able to provide. The same is true of your gifts. God has equipped you to do what no one else can do in exactly the same way as you can.

Paul explained this well to the Christians at the church in Corinth when he wrote to them about this matter. Using the human body as an analogy, Paul said,

> If the foot should say, "Because I am not a hand, I am not of the body," is it therefore not of the body? And if the ear should say, "Because I am not an eye, I am not of the body," is it therefore not of the body? If the whole body were an eye, where would be the hearing? If the whole were hearing, where would be the smelling? But now God has set the members, each one of them, in the body just as He pleased. And if they were all one member, where would the body be? But now indeed there are many members, yet one body. And the eye cannot say to the hand, "I have no need of you"; nor again the head to the feet, "I have no need of you." (1 Cor. 12:15–21)

Finding Your Way

It is important to keep in mind that we need not fear that somehow we might miss discovering God's will for our lives. He does not
dangle it somewhere up there in the spiritual realm, waiting to see if
we are committed enough or clever enough to figure it out. Quite the
contrary. Discovering God's calling happens easily when we are seeking how best to serve him in day-to-day matters and when we are
obeying his Word. His plan for each of us naturally unfolds as we put
his Word into practice where we are, where he has placed us, today.

But, like Olivia, we are still faced with questions about all the competing alternatives. How can you determine which course is the best
one? Perhaps you do not know what you are good at and what spiritual
gifts you possess. Your friends, family, and those who know you best can
be helpful in enabling you to determine what those are. Is there a particular aspect of your character or personality for which you frequently
are given compliments or for which your service is sought? In Olivia's
case, she has often been asked to fill in for absent teachers, even at the
college level. That has helped reinforce her understanding of the gifts
and talents she possesses. As a result, Olivia is beginning to realize that
perhaps God is calling her to pursue work in an academic setting and
to make use of her teaching gifts in church as well.

Are you someone others turn to in times of trouble, seeking a listening ear and a word of encouragement? If that is the case, your gifts likely
lie along those lines. Perhaps you are not socially inclined, and you prefer activities that involve less interaction with people. Rather than forc-
ing yourself into a career or area of service within the church that requires
constant face-to-face interaction, work with what you have. Seek ministry tasks and jobs that enable you to serve behind the scenes.

Maybe, like Lydia, you are an independent woman who loves new
challenges and interaction with all sorts of people. If so, a career or
service for Christ that keeps you confined behind a desk all day would
prove to be frustrating, as well as preventing others from benefiting
from what you have to offer. How do you feel when friends drop by

your home unannounced? Many of us find it an irritating interruption, but others love such spontaneous social encounters. If you enjoy guests at all different times, you may have the gift of hospitality as Lydia did. If you love domesticity and entertaining in your home, you can use that for God's glory by providing a thoughtful, warm, and caring environment for the lonely or others in need.

Another indicator of your calling is personal desire. Desire is a frequent tool that God uses to get us where he wants us to live and serve. Often we are suspicious of our desires, fearing that somehow if we want something, it cannot possibly be something that God wants for us. But that is not so! The desire to pursue a certain path, so long as it does not violate biblical principles, is often initiated in our hearts by God. You are free to make any choice that is not biblically forbidden. That means that you do not need to fret about whether pursuing a career in teaching or nursing is God's will or whether you should serve your church as a deaconess or by leading a Bible study. The choices we make within the framework of Scripture are the working out of our personal callings.

Begin to thank God for how he has made you. Even those things you would like to change about yourself are no accident but in keeping with God's design for how you are to glorify him. Your looks, your personality, even the quirky things about you, all work to the glory of God. And when you seek to discover and embrace them fully, you will find to your eternal pleasure that you are contributing to the upbuilding of the body of Christ as well as to your own happiness.

Romans 12 confirms the way for you to find and use your unique gifts. There Paul wrote, "I beseech you therefore, brethren, by the mercies of God, that you present your bodies a living sacrifice, holy, acceptable to God, which is your reasonable service. And do not be conformed to this world, but be transformed by the renewing of your mind, that you may prove [that is, live out and experience for yourself] what is that good and acceptable and perfect will of God" (Rom. 12:1–2). Will you do it? That is what Lydia did, and because she did, her gifts and talents have been marked for all time.

Notes

Chapter 3: Hagar: Where Freedom Is Found

1. James Montgomery Boice, *The Minor Prophets, Two Volumes in One* (Grand Rapids, Mich.: Kregel, 1996), 230.

Chapter 7: Dinah: The Boredom Blues

1. For more on living within God's sovereignly drawn boundary lines, read Dean R. Ulrich, "Lines in Pleasant Places: Joshua 15:19," *The Journal of Biblical Counseling* 18, no. 3 (spring 2000): 54–57.

Chapter 12: Hannah: Forget Me Not

1. James Montgomery Boice, *Romans*, volume 4, *The New Humanity* (Grand Rapids, Mich.: Baker, 1995), 1559.

Chapter 15: Gomer: A Real Heartbreaker

1. For much of my insight on the downward slope of sin, I am indebted to the teaching on Hosea by James Montgomery Boice, *The Minor Prophets, Two Volumes in One* (Grand Rapids, Mich.: Kregel, 1996).

2. Ibid., 17.

Chapter 16: Mary: Attaching the *Extra* to *Ordinary*

1. Theologians refer to Mary's words of praise as the Magnificat, from its opening word in the Latin version.

2. J. I. Packer, *Knowing God* (Downers Grove, Ill.: IVP, 1973), 247.

Chapter 17: Anna: Far from Over

1. David Powlison, *Dynamics of Biblical Change* (Philadelphia: Westminster Theological Seminary & C.C.E.F., 1995), 49.

Chapter 20: The Samaritan Woman: Satisfaction Guaranteed

1. James Montgomery Boice, *The Gospel of John*, volume 1, *The Coming of the Light, John 1–4, Living Water* (Grand Rapids, Mich.: Baker, 1999), 278.

2. Taken from Geoffrey T. Bull, *God Holds the Key* (London: Hodder and Stoughton, 1967), 70–71.

Index of Scripture